# The Fish Finder Chronicles

Volume One: Arriving through Pickleball

By A. J. Fraties

ISBN: 978-1-7322529-0-5

ISBN: 978-1-7322529-1-2 (ebook)

With love to all my family,
both relatives and pickleball family.

# Acknowledgments

Contributions to this first volume of *The Fish Finder Chronicles* have come from many people. Their encouragement kept me going, and their straightforward but good-natured criticism has been invaluable.

First and foremost is always my wife, Irene. She is my sounding board, my alter ego, and my prime collaborator. Thanks also to Prem Carnot, Roger Fellows, Mark Friedenberg, John Grasso, Rodney Grubbs, Al Hager, Wayne Kennedy, Gale Leach, Steve McDonough, Lee Moore, Verna Moore, Mark Nelson, Marian Pasela, Rosemary Reese, Les Scott, and Palm Creek's Senior Pickleball Philosopher, Noel White. And a major shout-out to my editor, Jami Carpenter. Her sense of humor and eye for my errors were magnificent.

You don't have to know where you're going
to get exactly where you need to go.

~ Marilyn A. Hepburn

# Introduction

You don't have to know much about pickleball to read this book, but in places it wouldn't hurt to know a little. Briefly, pickleball is a sport played on a court that measures 20 feet by 44 feet. It can be played by two or four players (singles and doubles). The game looks a little like miniature tennis, in that opponents face each other across a net in the middle.

Equipment consists only of paddles, which look like oversized table-tennis paddles, and a plastic ball about 3" in diameter with between 26 and 40 holes.

Points can only be won by the serving team and games are (with some exceptions) to 11 points, win by two points. A unique feature of a pickleball court is called the Non-Volley Zone or (more usually) the kitchen. The kitchen is an area that extends across the width of the court seven feet back from the net on either side. Players can go into the kitchen but cannot volley a ball that hasn't yet bounced while they're in the kitchen. Doing so is a fault (foot fault). Remember that term.

Pickleball is considered one of the fastest-growing sports in the United States and perhaps in the world. Once the provenance of geezer-jocks, the game is now played at its highest levels by the younger generation, assuring its continued development. Please go to Pickleball.Biz, the USA Pickleball Association, or search YouTube to learn more about this terrific game.

By the way, you follow any implied advice about playing pickleball at your own risk. The sport is difficult enough to master as it is.

Just sayin'.

# Chapter One

*DON'T THINK ABOUT IT,* thought Jon 'Fish' Fisher. *Clear your mind,* he thought. *Two points,* he reminded himself. *One at a time. Don't think about it.*

As he and Kirk worked their way back up the losers' bracket, he had felt all the old sensations coming back. His left arm, his serving arm, seemed noticeable, detached almost, not natural. His left hand felt heavy. The paddle didn't fit in his hand correctly. The feeling was very weird, unnatural. His serve was going away again.

Losing his serve always came on in stages, escalating as he paid more attention to its progression. At the beginning, he was still okay. He could self-talk his way through it, using the tools he had worked on. Visualizing where the serve would land had a place, as did diaphragmatic breathing. But now, 13-11 in the gold medal tie-breaker, only two points away from winning the 4.0 bracket, he felt like he had never served a pickleball before. Like he was in someone else's bad dream. Like he was using somebody else's body to do something he had done thousands of times before, but now couldn't.

Fish called time out, put his paddle over the ball in the right court, and walked to the fence where Kirk was standing.

Kirk looked at him. "You good?" he asked.

"No," said Fish. "I'm not." He could feel his breaths, too

9

shallow, too quick. He felt a bit light-headed, almost dizzy.

Kirk looked at him. "When you don't think about it, you serve great," he said simply. "So do it!"

"Right," Fish said. "Right." A side-out ago, instead of hitting the ball with his grooved serve, a nice, simple, single-step bowling stroke, he had pivoted on the ball, turning it over so far right that it shot sideways off his racket face and had, in fact, bounced over the fence between the courts near the net line.

"Geeze, Jon," Kirk said, irritated. "We've worked on this. We've got these guys. We get any two points and it's Miller Time. Just get the ball in play!" That was the longest speech Fish had heard him make.

At time-in, Fish took the ball and tossed it up, supposedly to see how much wind there was. There was no wind, it was dead-calm, but like most players, he always worked a pre-serve routine. Today, however, the routine did nothing to calm his anxiety. He felt the old familiar buzzing, like his head was connected to an electrical outlet. He breathed with his diaphragm ... three times. He dropped the ball with his right hand, and suddenly didn't know what to do next. Literally. He had to do something. He took a stab at the ball. It hit the paddle's edge guard, went straight up in the air and came to rest in the kitchen, two feet short of the net.

Written somewhere is an old adage: You don't get the ball in, you're gonna lose. Which they did. 13-15. Close, but no cigar.

As they were leaving the court, Kirk, master of few words, used a few. "You better find a serve, Fish. That was messed up."

Fish knew exactly what Kirk meant. Kirk could be a good partner for him, but not right now, not until he could get the serve in. But under pressure, how to do it? That was a question he couldn't answer.

He couldn't answer it years ago in college when the same issue — losing his serve under pressure — cost him his place on the varsity tennis team. And he couldn't answer it now. Besides visualizing where he would serve and trying to control his breathing, he had tried other types of serves. Backhand serves? No good. Granny-style between the legs? Worked sometimes, but the shame of having to do it was almost as bad as losing the serve to begin with. Right-handed instead of his normal left-handed? Not a prayer. Facing the opponent? Worse. Cross-over step, like Yoda Freidenburg? Nope. Not moving his feet? No good, no good.

Sometimes a new serve worked for a day or two. The most success he had had in regaining a functional serve was his adoption of the Pickleball Guru's sky-high lob serve. That worked for a week until he found that he could serve long quite well with it, and in fact, served one ball over the back fence to the amusement of the other three players on the court.

This was a game he wanted to play well. He wanted that a lot. And he knew, paradoxically, that wanting a serve so badly kept him from having one. But paradox or not, he couldn't play doubles without a partner and if he couldn't serve, nobody he could win with would partner with him.

Walking through the crowd with his head down, he had the strangest thought. *Do all these other guys have some kind of secret?* This was followed by another, *like some kind of power.* He shook his head. *Maybe I'm going crazy for real this time.*

# Chapter Two

FISH DRIFTED HIS RED KIA SOUL into the last parking spot in Dr. Samuel Blaskin's parking lot and smiled. Finding a parking spot in the good doctor's lot was a rare event. Even though Dr. Blaskin had only a small psychiatric practice and wasn't taking new patients these days, and his practice had boiled down almost to a hobby, by rights there should be a dozen spots open all the time. But Dr. Sammy also let his kids and grandkids park extra cars, trucks, ATVs, snowmobiles, and even boats in the other spaces. Many times over the year they'd been working together Jon wound up parking way, way down the street only to find no one at all in the waiting room.

He rooted in the backseat, found the manila folder, made sure the two yellow pages were on top before getting out.

It was overcast and calm in Bend and he took a minute to stare at the Ponderosa Pines ringing the parking lot, a fair amount of snow in their tailored branches. In between were more disheveled junipers and trimmed-up barberry bushes. Jon felt kindred for tall things and the pines were mature, maybe 40 feet. Fat gray squirrels and big Steller's jays were scrounging in the tree tops and scolding each other. Nice. Again, made him reflect on the plan. He'd miss all this.

He pushed open the carved wood office doors and saw Sarah, Dr. Sam's receptionist. Sarah was younger than

Fish, a good foot shorter and attractively plump. Her eyes were an extraordinary gray, beautiful eyes, really, but at the same time a bit direct-staring like a shark's. Her hair was mid-back length and brown. A good-looking woman.

Early on, Sarah had put something of a move on him, but nothing had developed. Jon was attracted to the opposite sex, but so far in his life had been pathetic with relationships. In fact, three years back, he had single-handedly ruined a very acceptable four-year marriage with a nice girl for reasons he still didn't understand. Since then he had only a very off-on relationship with a physical therapist in town, more like passing friends with occasional privileges, his time with her more like a workout than love.

Overall, Fish thought most of his relationship problems were his. For instance, he seldom realized someone was interested in him until way too late. Sarah was a perfect example. Things didn't end well with her. After she finally took offense over his total lack of response, she suddenly developed lockjaw when he was around, never smiling, never saying a spare word. He wasn't inconvenienced by this, except that on more than one occasion, his appointments had also disappeared. And in one case everyone disappeared; the office was closed and locked with a chain. Dr. Sam had given Fish a free appointment for that one.

Today Sarah was dressed in a mock camo jumpsuit, which made her look like a military policewoman. But it was a stylish outfit nonetheless that featured her legs, a real plus, and she was smiling at him, another plus.

"Hey, Sarah," he said. "Nice outfit. What's new?"

"Thanks, and same-old." She put a heavy black-polished nail to her lower lip, gave him a Mona Lisa smile. "But I heard somebody talking about you the other day!"

"Really! Who?" He was genuinely curious. Who would

talk about him?

"Wasn't the Doc. It was one of your pals at Bend Parks and Rec." That odd, knowing smile again. "Or should I say ... your soon-to-be-ex-pal?"

"What? Oh. Wow. Are you serious? Word is around already. Shoot!" He thought for a second, decided it didn't matter; he had quit, in fact. "Anyway ... thanks. Is he ready to see me?" He gestured toward the doctor's closed office door.

"Oh, sorry. He's running ten minutes late. Something about a grandkid's baseball practice. But," she said, looking off, "he said to go in and get comfortable. And he said he left something for you. He said it was important."

Fish's antennae went way up. Before this, neither Sarah nor Sam had ever suggested he go into the doctor's office alone. It didn't seem at all proper. And left him something? What would the good doctor leave him, besides a bill? But, hey, whatever. He nodded, opened the door, walked through to his usual seat. The armchair had a small envelope taped to the back. He peeked inside at a white 3x5 card that had 'Fish' written on it with a black Sharpie. Below his name was a small line-drawing of something, maybe the outline of road-kill with four feet and a long nose, and below that, 'Keep This Card!' Around the outline was pink highlighter, like fluorescent electrical rays coming off the drab road-kill.

Dutifully he pulled out the card, stared at it, then shoved it in a pocket and scrunched himself down into the overstuffed brown leather armchair. He drummed long fingers on the thick armrests and stared at nothing. After a while he stared past his shrink's empty chair at his diplomas on the wall. With his good eye he could only read the closest diploma: Samuel Blaskin, Master of Science, Honors, Gonzaga. With both eyes, last year, he could read all four. But that was last year, twenty-six visits

15

ago, and lots had changed since then.

In a few minutes Dr. Blaskin would come in for their last session, a year's journey. But what had Fish learned over the year? That he felt entirely rootless and unsettled in Bend, Oregon, the town he was born into? That suddenly he hated every minute he spent at Bend Parks and Rec, doing the job he'd previously loved for thirty-two years? That his first and only house, his blue Craftsman set in the middle of the downtown, a prime location nine minutes from work by bicycle, now felt like a ginger-breaded prison? That after fifty-two years he really had no friends to speak of, one divorce and certainly no significant other? That even his gentle parents, the two most supportive people he had ever known, settled now in their new digs at Rocky Ridge, triggered him to anger and sometimes to rage and tears? What was all this about?

So here he was again, dozens of visits and a year after coming in to see Doctor Blaskin. Fish thought he was perhaps less of a mess; thanks to Sam, he had labels for some of his discomfort. He even had a crazy plan. Sam had assigned him to come in with one today and he had. Not a great one, he knew, but at least it was a plan. But as to the why he was going through all this, all the new unpleasant emotions, all the emotional struggle, all of this was new and way beyond him. "Why screw up a good thing?" could have been his motto for the last couple of decades, really. And in his situation, it had all been good things for a good long time, at the very least good enough; all except his eye, of course.

But his eye, he felt, hadn't really triggered his angst, though it was the one thing about him physically that had changed. A chance accident, Karma, playing pickleball at the new Pine Nursery courts. How ordinary. Playing pickleball, he got hit in the eye, shattering his sunglasses, a shard piercing the inside edge of his left cornea, leaving that eye impaired. Various doctors had examined him.

The damage was entirely physical, not psychosomatic, the diagnosis was Optic Neuritis, a catch-all term. He had been tested for the occasional underlying causes of Optic Neuritis like MS; fortunately, all tests were negative. He might regain some or all of his vision, there was nothing, really, to operate on, only time would tell, blah, blah, blah … lots of doctor bullshit, no help. He didn't have a plan for this obstacle; he didn't even have a follow-up appointment.

Granted, this was a big deal in his life, but it had occurred after he had already begun melting down. It didn't seem to fit into the strum und drung he was dragging through, all the shit, all the anger and anxiety and even grief, all of which seemed to be related to nothing at all. Excepting God, if there was one, telling him to get out of Dodge.

Then there was this pickleball thing. After blowing out a perfectly good full-ride tennis college scholarship at OSU because his serve dissolved whenever he was in a close game, he tried to give up competitive sports entirely. And he had, for a couple of decades. Now, with a year under his belt on the smaller pickleball courts, he was competing again — and he believed he had a shot at greatness, or good-ness, at least. But his old problems in tennis seemed to have been waiting, and again his serve was erratic and difficult.

What the hell was he supposed to do with all this crap? What would a normal, non-crazy person do? And when, for that matter, had he actually become crazy? Highly creative, highly visual, yes. His flashes spoke to that; sporadic, non-predictable moments when he made synergistic connections that created something more than the sum of its parts. Able to make cray-cray connections maybe others didn't always make. Was that crazy? He didn't know. And what was an exploding animal drawn on a 3x5 card — he thought the black part must be an animal — supposed to mean to him?

## Chapter Three

"ARE YOU WITH US, FISH?" Dr. Blaskin asked, straight-faced, his heavy face and droopy jowls radiating only a little displeasure, which, Fish found, probably meant he was reasonably glad to see him.

"Sorry," Fish said, shaking off his reverie. "I didn't see you come in. Or sit down. You're pretty sneaky for a shrink."

"I think of myself more as an unassuming sanitary engineer, tip-toeing through piles of shit for a living." Blaskin removed his coke-bottle glasses and shined them with an awful green tie one son had given him two decades before. "Remember, I'm mainly here to help you clean that stuff out of your mind. Assuming it's possible after watching you lose your serve again Sunday."

"You saw that last match, huh?" Jon scowled, scrunched his tall frame down a bit lower, stuck his long lean legs under the heavy mahogany partner's desk.

"Yeah, I made the mistake of stopping by the courts instead of just going to the dog park. Wish I hadn't." The doctor held his nose, made the choking motion, hand on throat, with the other hand.

Fish gave him a bigger scowl.

"Not my job to fix you," said Blaskin. "Although I'm willing to help. Did you get the card?"

"Is this supposed to tell me something?" He pulled out and held up the card, waved it at the doctor. "All I can think of is something on fire under my house."

"And I think you're a moron," the doctor said kindly. "I recognize the dissatisfaction you've had with the lack of progress that, to your point, your insurance policy paid for. On the plus side, you've stopped arguing a lot of stuff with yourself in the last few weeks." The good doctor peered at him intently. "In fact, isn't today 'plan day'? Did you get your homework done? Can I fire you now?"

"Right. You don't want to talk about the card." Fish reached in his folder, pulling out the two yellow sheets. "Luckily, I do have a plan. I'm not sure how good it is, though. Can I go through it? Maybe ask some questions?"

"It's your 45 minutes," Samuel said, giving the 'whatever' wave. "And it's your insurance company's non-refundable money, which my grandkids need for their college tuition funds, so it's all good." He smiled agreeably.

Fish looked back at his plan. Basically, he thought of it as having two parts. Internal, what's inside him, his feelings, and external, like job, pickleball. Both were killing him. He looked down at his stained blue gym shorts before he spoke.

"Actually, I've been working on this plan all week," he hesitated, holding up the two pages, "but I haven't found a way to make it sane. You sure you wanna hear?"

"My breath is bated," the doctor agreed.

Fish had one of his flash moments — he flashed on the large man across from him, his lips pursed, a huge purple-brown night-crawler poking half its worm body out at the corner of his mouth like something from the movie *Beetlejuice*. Yow!

Fish took a deep breath, straightened up a little. Looked at his notes. "So. This is the plan. Two parts. Problem first. Second part, what I do to fix it, like we agreed."

He took another breath and began to read. "The problem," he said. "The problem is I don't know who I am any more. It's like I'm some kind of ghost, inhabiting my own body, not sure what it's gonna do next. And the longer I stay around Bend, the worse it's getting." He looked at the doctor.

"Needs work, it'll do," Sam said. "Say more."

"Okay, so doing all the same things I have always done and expecting different results is making me crazy."

Sam held up a hand. "Did I ever tell you Einstein's quote on that matter? 'We cannot solve our problems with the same thinking that caused them!'"

Fish looked at him and rolled his eyes. "Do you mind? Anyway, to do something new I gotta break some chains. So, first step, I quit my job. Second, I rent out my house. Third, I make sure the parents are okay, and let 'em know they've got to fend for themselves for a while."

Sam glanced up. "Well, I suppose those steps would address some of your weird feelings ..."

"I'm hoping," agreed Fish. "Then I buy an RV; I'm thinking I get a diesel pusher and learn to drive it. And I buy a car to tow with me." Even with bad vision he saw Sam's grimace. Sam was irrational about a fair number of things and motor homes, especially big-ass pushers, were very high on his list.

Fish felt himself getting into the swing a little. Another plus, no more flashes. The night-crawler was apparently back in the doctor's mouth, calming Fish somewhat.

"Then Ray and I go traveling. For a good long while, maybe." He dropped his eyes at his notes, took a breath. "And maybe I become a one-eyed professional pickleball player!"

21

Sam, who had been jotting notes furiously, stared at them for a minute. "Wow," he said, looking up at last. "I honestly don't know what to say. That's all quite remarkable. How did you make that many decisions in a week?"

"I just did what I said I'd do." Fish put a large palm forward to stop the doctor, who seemed to want to jump in on the 'doing what I said I'd do' part.

"I broke everything down. I took each piece that was bothering me. Losing my serve, just like in college. The boredom at my job. Coming to the same house every day, by myself, well, me and Ray. Seeing my parents almost every day. Them seeing me. Me always angry with them for what? No reason at all. Playing pickleball and figuring out how to do it with one eye but not being good enough even there 'cuz I'm not great and being bored 'cuz I'm not learning much else about it. Having a goal around pickleball. Is it stupid to have a pickleball goal? Maybe I'd do it so I'd feel like I have a reason to be out traveling around."

"And then ..." Sam urged.

"And then, middle of the night two nights ago, I was lying awake running through all that, reminding myself of every reason why all those steps were insane. This was like two hours of straight rumination, and maybe the third night in a row doing that, dragging through the next day like a zombie. But then I stopped fighting it. I accepted it.

"Accepted that I don't like what I'm doing. I've liked some of this all my life, or at least I thought I did, but I don't like it now. Basically, none of it. At the very least, if I don't like it, I can try to change it."

"Nobody can change it but you," Sam agreed. "And I like that you don't have any real answers to what's gonna come next. Man plans while God laughs. So ... what's your question?" he asked, sitting back, his heavy arms

22

crossed.

"Let's start with this, since you didn't answer before." He held up the card. "Why did you leave me this? What does it mean? Why should I care diddly-squat what this is?"

## Chapter Four

"IT WILL MEAN SOMETHING, I think," Dr. Sam said, picking at a cuticle. "To be honest, it may mean more than anything you've stumbled across in a long time."

Fish flashed, his word for his wild non-sequitur habit of making something truly nutty out of the ordinary he saw or heard. He saw the card metamorphosing into a real animal, the edges of the card assimilating slowly into its flesh. He saw the animal disintegrating, crumbling, re-assembling, He shook his head. "No, really! What kind is this? Is it a clue? A suggestion? Something your crazy receptionist drew and put on my chair?"

Sam patted his coat pocket and took out his phone. Turned it toward Fish. The wallpaper visible on the phone held a circle with a red outline of the same animal in the middle. It was an animated GIF …it blew up like fireworks, re-invented itself, did it again. "Well, for you, it's either all of something or part of something."

Fish shifted again, uncomfortable. "Maybe it's you who's crazy."

Sam took a while to answer, thinking, drumming thick fingers on the desk. For effect, Fish thought. The doctor fired up an old soup bowl briar that smelled like Fish's sweat socks. He pictured the sweat socks crawling out of his bag, crawling up Sam's face, changing into a pipe, emitting smoke. *I really need more sleep*, Fish thought. *Or fewer meds. Or more meds.*

"I don't think either one of us is crazy. What's remarkable," Sam said at last, waving at the huge cloud of vile blue smoke that didn't ever rise but hung around him like a shroud, "is not even how sane your plan is, which it is, but how complete it is. It doesn't sound crazy, not to me. Not at all."

Fish felt ridiculously pleased. He needed validation, especially from Sam who could always keep him, or at least GET him, grounded. "You sure about that?" he asked semi-casually.

Sam grinned. "Just to let you know, I see what you're doing there. But okay. You love your job, you know it's the one job you come out of college with that a recreation degree and a minor in art allows you to help people play, allows you to design, have artistic expression in a practical application. Am I right?"

"Sure. That's why I stayed there three friggin' decades! Love the play, love the art ..."

"But for ... what ... over a year in here, you've been talking about how bored you are, how you've had weird feelings of running amuck in the midst of the headquarters building on Columbia, dreaming of crapping right on the tile in the foyer in front of the reception desk?" Sam checked off the items in the air with his pencil.

"You've been paying attention to how crazy I am; so what?"

"So, in the plan you address all that, somehow, and you just leave the job. With your seniority at Bend Parks and Rec. you have a good pension, am I right? So your finances should be okay. Or should I say 'finances are okay.' You're already retired, aren't you?"

Fish nodded, feeling a bit sheepish. "Yeah, the money

works, and yeah, I retired two days ago." He leaned across at Sam. "How did you know?" he asked suspiciously.

Sam waved the remark away. "Sarah, of course. Heard it someplace and told me. She knows everything." He created another eruption of smoke, farted noisily, shifted his seat. "'Scusa. Riced cauliflower for lunch."

"But back to the plan ..." Fish prompted.

"Yep." He glanced down at his notes. "Second step. You love your house but then again, it's the only place you've lived in ... what ... thirty years? So you have to get away from it for a while, which makes sense to me, by the way. But you're not talking about selling it, keeping your options open for later."

"And my parents are good right now ..." added Fish, waving his hand in a circle, hurrying it along.

"Yeah, you've got very little family, so it's natural you're concerned about their well-being. And they don't need your money. I know Sam and Bernice and if you had their money you could throw yours away and you know that, too. Plus, they're loving Rocky Ridge; it's an outstanding place. It's like a resort. Emily and I are even considering it for ourselves, buying a place now, be ready in a few years."

"Huh!" said Fish. "You never mentioned that before."

"You do remember it's only about you in here, but outside here, I do have a life, right?" He smiled. "Anyway, your parents are fine and you'll be able to come back when they aren't."

Sam continued. "The one thing I wonder about is why you decided to follow pickleball instead of become a bird-watching fanatic or something. Clearly pickleball's a big part of your life these days. But at its core it's just another competitive sport and we've talked forever about you and competitive sports; they don't always agree with you and your stomach, am I right?"

Fish shrugged and nodded. "Yeah, it's the losing thing. I threw away a close match Sunday and didn't puke, so I guess that's progress, but I hated losing it so much! Same old crap; felt like a nail driving through my stomach."

"And the AFib ..." The doctor waited. When Fish had an attack of self-loathing on the court it usually ratcheted his heart rate through the ceiling, which naturally kicked in his atrial fibrillation as well.

Fish nodded. "Yeah, there's that. But it's all that stuff I never got fixed in tennis, y' know?"

"So, ignoring those two things for a moment, here's why you're a moron."

Fish flashed, a picture of comedian Jeff Foxworthy coming into his mind unbidden, saying, "You might be a redneck ... no, make that a moron ..."

The doctor was moving on. "Some plans are based on imperatives, things people have to do. They lose their home, they make a plan, find somewhere else to live. In your case, most of the pieces of your plan are simply choices between positives. Also, most people find they have to do something different at some point. Need to make different choices. You're what — 52? Took you a little longer than most, is all."

Fish nodded. "Okay, I get I'm making choices and that feels right. But I mean, it's such an upsetting plan. So non-linear? Upsetting like in turning everything upside down?"

"That's just you labeling things, and anyway I think plans are simply alternative ways of measuring reward against risk." Dr. Blaskin held his two meaty palms above his desk, moving them up and down like a scale, weighing things. "And really, what's the worst thing that could happen?"

Bam. Flash. Unbidden, Fish saw himself on a park bench now, down at Drake Park, covered with newspapers and snow, his pup Ray under the bench, shivering, protecting his ratty sleeping bag and his shopping cart. "Wrong? With this plan? Lots," said Fish. "Everything."

"Say more?" invited Sam.

"Park-bench scenario. I'd wind up with no job, no available house to live in, my parents would die when I was away, and I'd be a loser, probably throw up on the courts, come back here feeling like a fool. The shame alone would kill me, if I didn't starve first. Or freeze to death on my bench."

"Would you be bored?" Sam said, too casually. "Before you starved or froze, I mean."

"Probably not," admitted Fish, thinking about it. "Hard to be bored when you're terrified or starving or frozen."

"Yes, indeed! But, really, Jon. Could you starve? What with your retirement and rental income from your house?"

"Yes," Fish said, refusing the bait. Sam arched a bushy eyebrow at him. "Okay, no," Fish amended sheepishly.

"And is it likely that you wouldn't get back in time to help your parents if they got ill? Where would you be playing in tournaments? Uzbekistan?"

"No." Fish felt like a trap was closing on him, a trap he had sprung on himself somehow. "More like Arizona. That's where the big boys play. Mainly."

Sam looked at his silver Rolex, a present from his wife when he had announced his approaching retirement. "Big boys? The odds of you actually making it as a playing professional are slim-to-none."

"Fuck you very much!" Fish muttered, refusing to agree.

## Chapter Five

SAM WAS UNMOVED. "Anyway, to be blunt, life's been too easy on you the last decade or so. There's an urban legend that we only use 10 percent of our brain power. That's probably not literally true but it does imply we can change if we want. Fly, lose your attachment to being a caterpillar! And our time's about up, anyway."

"Whoa, wait," Fish stalled. "One more thing. Before, you said *almost* all the pieces in my plan are just choices I'm making. From my perspective, everything there was a choice."

"Largely unimportant, but since you ask ..." Sam smiled benevolently, standing across the desk, looking around for his phone. "You really didn't have any choice about leaving, did you? I'm sure you looked at every possible way to avoid this."

"Well, maybe if I had been using more than that 10 percent you talked about ..."

"If, if, if. I said that 10 percent thing is just an urban legend, but yeah, maybe," said Sam. "If it's true. And of course, you'd need to accomplish it. Otherwise, maybe not."

They walked together to the office door, shook hands, double-handed shakes, more than usual. "By the way, since you brought up suicidal urges and all, what am I supposed to do if I need help staying on track out there?"

Fish asked.

"You can always call me if you implode." Sam smiled up at Fish. "'Course, I'm not licensed outside of Oregon, so I can't bill, so I probably won't answer." The smile turned up into a grin for a second. "But that does bring up something."

"What?" Fish asked.

"Well, my opinion only … you need, like, a guide. You are enormously creative. You see connections, possibilities, stuff that other people never see. That flashing you do … that's something other people, other artists would kill for. That's creativity speaking to you, whether or not you want to hear it. Or understand it. That's good, but it can drive you crazy, not knowing which way to turn. You're gonna be out there on your own. So, I agree, you need a person to keep you on track, moving toward a different life. Somebody who doesn't tell you what to do, but one who doesn't just allow you to get caught up in a different version of what you're doing here. A life coach or something. Someone who can help you move past 10 percent."

"Well, that was you, at least here," added Fish, seeing where this was going.

"It was, sort of." Sam clapped him heavily as they walked. "But no mas. I'm a friend of yours, and a decent shrink, but I'm only licensed in Oregon. Doesn't really make for my being a good life coach when you're off in Bumfuck, Egypt."

"So what do I do? Just wait? 'When the student is ready the master will appear?'" Fish didn't feel comfortable with waiting for anything at this point.

"So, I've made a call." The doctor was straight-faced. "To get things started. You don't have to thank me."

"You already made a call? About my life coach? Isn't that

something I should do?" Fish asked, annoyed.

"Nope, 'cuz you wouldn't. Anyway, don't worry, he'll find you."

"He? C'mon, Sam, this isn't right. Who is he, why do I want to use him, and how will I even recognize him?"

"Well, to the last part, you'll definitely know who he is, even if you don't immediately get it. And remember the card I gave you," he added. "If you have the card, you'll have a clue. That's really important!"

"Could you possibly be any more vague?" Fish asked, his cheeks flushing.

"A gift," admitted Sam. "I do have a hint for you, however. Your pickleball serve you need to work on out there? That's internal. But you will also have something external to address. You'll figure it out. It's a power thing."

They arrived at the Kia. "New," the doctor observed. "Huh. A little small. Like the clown car at the circus."

Flash ... literal, like doctor said, five of them, him the shortest, the last guy massive, like Shaq in clown paint. Getting in his Kia in the parking lot and settling in, Fish felt it, he was smiling. *With friends like him*, he thought, leaving the rest unsaid.

He drove past the doctor, who was getting into his old grey Subaru. Rolled down his window. "Funny. You know, I had this weird thought after I blew that Sunday match. Like I needed to develop some special power just to get a serve in. Then just now, you mentioned a power thing?"

Dr. Blaskin didn't turn; waved him away. "There may be something to that," he said over his shoulder. "But you may want to wait and see what develops."

Fish headed out of the parking lot, thinking about special

serving powers. About how to flat-tow the Kia. Thinking about who the hell he was going to meet in Arizona. If he was. Thinking about teaching Ray, his boxer, to love the RV. Thinking about the drawing on the card and about finding some stranger who'd help him work on his life. Thinking about how to meditate, and from there monkey-minding to dying in the midst of a meditation sitting. "What the hell kind of a final session would that be, anyway?" he wondered, turning for home.

# Chapter Six

IT TOOK FISH MUCH longer than he thought it should to get on the road. He had been delayed by life — necessary things like finding the right RV, outfitting it, installing a brake-assist on the Kia, getting renters for his home. At last he and Ray were at the take-off point, their initial shake-down run to Arizona. Tryin' out the life, livin' large. After just a few days, they arrived at the Palm Creek Golf and RV Resort, home of the largest single-location pickleball facility in the country and home of a couple of the more recent USA Pickleball Association Nationals. Ray and he, safe and sound, ready for adventure.

The day was balmy, a Sunday in early March. The 'Duel in the Desert' Pickleball Tournament was underway. Fish was lucky and had even picked up a partner last minute — Jeff, a pretty solid soft-game-guy, and what're the odds of that? As a result, Fish was actually playing in the day's 4.0 skill-level men's doubles.

This was by far the biggest pickleball tournament Fish had seen. While certainly smaller than the Nationals or the U.S. Open, this was a major, no small potatoes. The Duel in the Desert was one of a small handful of Tier-Two USAPA pickleball tournaments, ranked largely by number of participants, and the players were everywhere, with spectators to spare. Probably 750 participants, twice that in spectators, spread out over four days.

To Fish's half-educated eye, the players all seemed good. The 4.0 bracket he was playing in, one he was an average-sized fish in up in Bend's pond, was more like Bend's 4.5+ bracket, meaning it was way tough. These 4.0s could play. There was no real difference, in Fish's mind, between Palm Creek's 4.0s and Bend's elite, the 4.5s and even some 5.0s, the top of the local ladder. They all knew all the shots, knew when to execute. If he forced himself to pay attention, about the only things making a difference between the brackets were consistency and patience. Well ... and age. The younger guys were better.

True, the 5.0s, even Bend's, could sometimes seem a bit super human and many could hit through concrete, but even there, their games were about the same. Same patterns of play, just better reactions, got everything back over the net, seemed in some magical way to be ready for anything. Fish ruminated a bit on his plan's objective, which was to play at the (Senior) Professional level. While these guys (both male and female) were still formally 'ranked' as being 5.0, they seemed to play above 5.0. Way above. Way, way above in some cases. Where he was sitting, looking down into the four sunken courts known as the Pit, Jon had watched Scott Irish manhandle his own opponent, 'Black' Steele, no small shakes himself, in Senior Professional Singles only a few minutes before, for example. And he thought he might get there? Be able to play against those guys? What was he smoking?

Fish sat on the top of the aluminum bleachers outside the pickleball courts, first watching the players in the Pit, then watching the other tournament players and the milling spectators. Afternoon temperatures were in the 70s, sunny, near cloudless. The tiniest breeze moved the American and Canadian flags on the court fence posts, not enough to give direction to the rainbow-colored windsocks hanging limp above the flags, but a little. For Fish, a big-time college tennis star back in the day, major pickleball tournaments like this one seemed similar to his tennis outings, but there were differences, so it was bright and new.

Fish and Jeff had lost their first match, no blowout, two close games, but a blemish on an otherwise enjoyable day. He still hated losing, hated not having a reliable serve. It still made his stomach turn over. He wasn't the guy on the college tennis team with his head in the locker-room trashcan throwing up before the match. He was the guy who threw up after they lost. Dr. Blaskin had trial-ballooned his diagnosis as performance anxiety during one session, but Jon pointed out he wasn't anxious about performing. He was anxious about losing.

Characteristically, Dr. Blaskin told him to suck it up and be anxious and afraid of losing but do it on his own time, not let his actions fuel his neurosis. "Most people are scared of losing," Sam had observed. "Granted, not as afraid as you, but then, you're special!"

Fish had rolled his eyes at him. "As in special needs," he asked, "right?"

"Yes," Sam had nodded agreeably. "Like that."

Being the tallest guy around, even sitting, his shaved head brushed the overhang of the green canvas shade structure directly above him and tickled, felt nice. His old blue sweatshirt was folded to cushion his bony butt, his wide shoulders rubbed now and then against tight-packed neighbors. He sat erect, head up, his white hat with the black circle in his lap, rubbing its brim absently with his fingers. Below him in the Pit the better players were battling, but he scarcely noticed. He felt something pleasant …was it peaceful? Not a familiar feeling for him, not these days. And it felt very good. "Nearly perfect," he breathed out, saying it softly.

The grey-haired woman sitting against him, maybe 60-ish, still athletic-looking, glanced at his profile sideways, offered a slight smile, leaned into him a tiny bit. To Fish she looked good, a bit too old for him, perhaps, but nicely put together, not many wrinkles, hair a mix of grey and blonde tied severely back in a mid-length ponytail, maybe dressed a bit prim for pickleball in her matching green tennis outfit and grey-green shoes, push-worthy for sure. He pushed back, friendly-like. They both smiled to themselves, facing ahead, keeping their options open.

Clothing in pickleball is flexible; it ain't lawn-bowling with everyone wearing whites on Friday. Really, there is no dress code except for wearing safe shoes. To Fish, pickleball was a backyard sport, so he could and did wear what he wore to work ... say ... in his garden, except for different shoes. Today he was a bit monochromatic; plain gray nylon shorts, a darker gray sleeveless top with a meaningless but oriental-looking red motif that, color-wise, matched his PaddleTek paddle, his white Gamma hat with its black circle, his only real colors being his silver-pewter neck medallion and his shoes, his metallic-looking K-Swiss Lozan Lii shoes, glinting like a metallic rainbow. Silly shoes he had bought on a whim ultra-cheap, barely used, size 14, off Ebay. They were magic shoes, like the PF Flyers his parents bought him years ago. He wouldn't give them up for hundreds now.

In spite of good intentions, his mental gymnastics started kicking in again. This thing he'd tried to say to himself, that perfect — like losing — was all in his mind. *What is perfect for me?* he wondered for the hundredth time. In theory it was family and friends and safety and warmth. And competition and winning. That's what perfect might be for Fish. All those things. Pickleball helped him be away from Bend, his home, helped him have a framework for being out in the larger world searching for something, some unspecified power, without looking too much like a dork while he did it. Maybe.

Of course, he still hid behind his mask. He even had an

'elevator speech' now that seemed to work when sitting around the late afternoon daily wine-fests outside one RV or another at this RV park. When it came his turn to introduce himself he told part of the truth. "I'm Fish, I'm retired, and I want to be a professional pickleball player when I grow up," he'd say. Most everybody there was a pickleball player so everybody would laugh, especially since Fish was about a light year or more away from being a superior player in the big-fish pond of Palm Creek.

And while most of the folks here were strangers, they were "just friends I haven't met yet," remembering his Will Rogers. Everyone around him, players, vendors, volunteers, spectators ... all could be part of his pickleball family. Almost like real family. Almost like friends, anyway. Almost perfect. Good enough, he thought.

Coming back from his mental masturbation to sitting on his aluminum seat, out of the waking dream, it was all so comfortable, with his eyes closed against the sun. Definitely he was not sleeping, just sitting. Watching with his inner eye. Flashes went through him, whole pictures and streams of consciousness, connections came and went. The player who walked by very near to him was female by her step, smelled strongly of body odor. He let that image float through for sure.

But ... maybe the feeling of comfort wasn't enough. Something itched at him, not physically. He tried to let the dissatisfaction go. No good. He was comfortable, but restless, too. Why? Maybe his and Jeff's first match? Two reasonably close games against the team he thought were the best players in the bracket. Shame. "If I had poached more ... or less?" He shrugged, loosened his shoulders, pulling them way back, opening his chest. He tried something simpler: followed his breath, asking his pulse to drop, his heart to slow. Trying to let shame, if shame it was, he wasn't sure, just go away. Jon, with his extraordinary monkey-mind, couldn't do it. But trying made him feel at least a little better.

Everyone has fear, everyone has anxieties; of course Fish knew that. But Fish hated fear. Fear was the precursor to anger, and anger often led to losing. And losing opened the door to the burning shame, the looks from other people, his teammates turning away, his parents telling him it was okay when he knew it wasn't, that's for damn sure ... not just in pickleball, he was new to it, only a year or so into it. A new fanatic. *That's what pickleball does to people,* he thought. Makes fanatics out of them.

## Chapter Seven

LOSING MOST OF THE USE of his left eye some ten months ago had changed Fish, no question. An unfortunate and random pickleball accident, for sure; an unsettling loss, of course. He might get some or all or none of his vision back. Nobody knew.

He always had a quick trigger but now not so much. The underlying anger hadn't gone away. But the competitiveness that characterized him from grade school to retirement was strangely quiet.

He needed to find something, maybe somebody to talk to. He had called around, found Dr. Samuel. Sam was a practicing psychotherapist, and among his acquaintances rated as one of the foremost meditation practitioners in Bend. Dr. Sam was also half Buddhist. Over the several months his moral code had begun to rub off on Fish. Didn't calm him down but made him focus more on the actual events. "See the ball," Sam would say, talking about the yellow ball that had tagged his eye, said while they sat quarter-lotus in his office. "Feel the anger," he said. Again, too easy to say, not easy to do. "Let the anger pass through. Allow it to change." Same thing; sounds good, doesn't work that well.

Finally, in one session, Fish asked, "Is this immersion therapy we're doing?"

Sam, caught out, nodded. "Does that bother you?" he asked.

"Nope," said Fish. "But I think I've been immersed enough. I'm good." And so they stopped talking about it. Of course, few things are ever truly settled or gone in the psyche, and once in a while, at first more often but then thankfully less frequently, the ball would come rocketing at him again and he'd feel the white-hot pain of plastic piercing his eye.

Now in Arizona waiting for his next match, practicing mental stuff, Fish did a body scan: followed his breath, took inventory. Thought about his eye. Felt his eye with his breath. All good. He fondled the pewter medallion, his mom's going-away gift to him, the infinity sign, customized with a brighter silver cross across its middle, hanging on the black leather cord she wove, resting quietly against his chest. Still not quite right. *Listen*, he thought. He put focus on his breath, its patterns. Nothing worked. His mind jumped from subject to subject like a frog moving across lily pads.

In college Fish had taken an elective course on Buddhism and learned the structure of several meditation practices. He didn't think he was good at any of them, judged in fact that he sucked, although of course part of the point was not to judge himself. "That's why we call it 'practice,'" Sam had said. But sucking at it or not, listening was a favorite meditation exercise for Fish. So he switched now from trying to focus on breath to trying to focus on noise.

He listened far out at first, hearing the drone of traffic and occasional sirens a mile off on Highway 10, hearing the clopping of the helicopters coming in and out from the hospital a block away, hearing the crop dusters — in his mind he saw them as bright yellow — spraying the growing white cotton plants, acres of them, rolling up almost to the highway. He tried to let the image pass across his mind and fade away like clouds against a clear blue sky. This would, of course, be great if it worked, but the image clicked by in 1/1000 of a second, a camera's shutter speed, and then jolted him back to some other place.

Okay, that didn't work. Changing it up, he tried bringing the listening in closer. In some ways this was even worse. Sitting in the middle of the sports complex, he heard all 32 courts, several dozen plastic pickleballs pock-pocking against paddles, a rapid, steady cacophony, like medium-hard rain on his motor home's fiberglass roof. It was a sound punctuated by occasional laughter, twice a round of applause, once the word "SHIT!" yelled way too loud, a young woman's sour voice sweetened by the crowd's laughter. The edges of Fish's full lips curved up; he imagined a glass swear jar, her sweaty hand stuffing in a wrinkled dollar. From the tip jar his mind jumped to a beer mug and from there to a beer bar he liked in downtown Bend. This wasn't working terribly well. Okay, this wasn't working at all. He brought the focus in even closer.

*This is impossible,* he thought, but that didn't make it uninteresting. Fish found himself the center of a mental movie in an imaginary theatre. First he heard the spectators near him, and, of course, the announcer. Every few seconds it was the same order, first speaker-crackle announced the announcement, then the broadcast: the next court assignment, the players, the referee, then the on-deck folks. This announcer was super good, had a real radio voice, deep, melodious, straightforward, and believable, with both intended and practiced inflections.

Meditation wasn't working, but Fish found himself amused by his imaginings. Obviously Mr. Announcer was busy, lots of courts and tons of matches meant he was very busy indeed, but he still found time to pitch the tournament sponsors and the night's free players' dinner, reminded players to check their goodie bags for their raffle ticket, mentioned the raffle drawing in an hour, exhorted players and spectators to "Get r-r-r-r-eady for ma-a-a-a-jor prizes, " trilling it way-way out like that guy in the WWE, adapting his "Let's get r-r-r-r-eady to r-r-r-u-m-m-ble." All the noises were irregular but blended together when Fish let them, separating them from time to time and trying to listen to one with more focus. A nice smorgasbord of noise, really, but hardly peaceful and settling.

He was reminded suddenly of an old joke: *A Buddhist monk walks up to a hotdog stand. 'Make me one with everything,' he said.* Fish smiled to himself; his ability to meditate might suck but he still had it, baby, Boop-Oop-a-Doop.

The crackling speakers prefaced the next new announcement. "Aardvark Rinpoche," the speakers squawked, "to Court One. Second call! Singles, 50-65 age, 4.0 bracket. Aardvark, to Court One, your match is waiting!"

He heard a slight urgency in Mr. Announcer's voice, but Fish was instantly charmed. Pickleball players often choose their names; he chose his, Fish, at least he sort of chose it, but Aardvark? Really? Someone playing with the name Aardvark? He flashed, of course. A real aardvark playing on a court? Waddling around? Or is that an armadillo or an anteater? Wonderful! He had to see this.

Fish opened his grey eyes, took a last calming breath, stood and stretched, arms above his head, chicken-winged his stretch against the shade structure, rubbed his sweating scalp, and climbed more or less gracefully down from the bleachers, pulling on his cap as he went.

He wended his way through the throngs of players and spectators, working farther south down the breezeway. Courts One and Two were at the end and against a sound wall, Court One being an inside court and away from the spectators. Even Fish, at his height, found it hard to get an unobstructed view of the inside court from the outside breezeway.

Once again Fish climbed up to the top of adjoining courtside bleachers, making it up easily enough. He now saw the whole of Court One. Fish looked over the two players warming up. One of them was ordinary-looking for a pickleball player, maybe a bit shorter than average, maybe dressed a little fancier – tropical green and grey board shorts, yellow and black court-friendly shoes, wife-beater 'T' in a subdued green, PaddleTek on its back, red and black Bantam PaddleTek paddle in hand. Probably a more experienced player, not a sponsored player if he was playing 4.0, only a moderate skill level, an ordinary guy, but he had his dress code down, that was for damn sure.

The other player wasn't ordinary. At all. If there was any doubt before, Fish had none now; this was the Aardvark. In a sport made up of different characters and appearances, Aardvark would stand out anywhere.

"Anywhere," Fish said out loud and vehemently. The guy next to him shot him a glance. "Sorry," Fish said. The guy next to him was almost as tall but much skinnier. He wore a taupe shirt with some animal on it, and Fish wanted take a closer look; something about the shirt design was familiar, but Aardvark called his attention. The very first thing was a real game-changer. This Aardvark guy was wearing a robe. No, *darn me*, he was PLAYING in a robe.

Not a bathrobe or a smoking robe. Not an academic robe, either. A wizard's robe? Not striking enough, although the color — orange — was unusual, like a monk, Fish guessed. Okay, so maybe it really was a monk's robe, although Fish thought one hardly ever saw a player wearing a religious robe on a pickleball court. This was a guess; he hadn't been around pickleball all that much. But he never saw anyone playing even in a bathrobe before, that was also for damn sure.

He squinted and peered; it was a light robe but the

material was expensive looking, held mostly together with a wide taupe sash. It billowed and flowed around thick brown legs as he charged after shots, most of which he missed. When he pivoted, the back of the robe went straight like it was ironed. Jon thought there was a design on the back. Subtle, barely visible at this distance, but maybe an infinity sign, like on his medallion, although it seemed more compressed and rounder, like a Mobius Strip, a strip with one continuous side, Fish remembered, flashing back to entry-level physics at OSU. Chinese robes sometimes have infinity signs on them, don't they? *No*, he answered himself, *they don't*. Was the A-vark Chinese? Fish thought not but probably people who weren't Chinese could wear a Chinese robe. Probably no law against it. Except nobody did it on a pickleball court, except, now, the Aardvark. He did. 100 percent, sample of one.

Fish dressed like he was near homeless, but he had some fashion sense, and he thought the Aardvark's shorts looked okay except for their color, a different orange, not like the robe. Not a rich orange, for sure. Sort of shiny, a plastic-y Walmart-Halloween-pumpkin orange. His shirt was white with a red and vaguely oriental design, complex; Fish couldn't tell what the design was. The shirt could be torn under one heavy arm, Fish couldn't tell that for sure, either, the robe being mostly in the way. The oriental design could have been an animal. He glanced again at the guy sitting next to him, his shirt. Yeah, it could be the same design. It also could be the design on the card, he thought. Huh!

This was a most colorful outfit, colorful like bright and also colorful like interesting, except for the A's shoes; these seemed to be ordinary old-school black and white tennis shoes, not court shoes but high-tops more like basketball shoes, yet without any style. They looked brand new, so clean the contrast between their white laces and black canvas gleamed like neon against a black wall. His socks appeared to be ribbed dark blue dress socks, close to knee-high, another thing you seldom saw on a court. *Could be compression socks,* Fish thought. *No,* he decided. A flash, two diabetics appeared in the theater of his mind, old, hunched over, wearing thigh-high white compression socks and jockstraps, no shorts, no shoes, playing singles. That, besides being just wrong in every way, also wasn't correct. *Dress socks,* the F decided. That's what they were. Ribbed dress socks.

Physically the Aardvark was short, not Little Person short, but noticeably so, maybe 5'5" or so, Fish guessed. But if things were proportional, based on his width, he was 7' tall; he was as wide as a barrel. Not fat, not thin, just wide and … thick. He was really, really thick everywhere — trunk, legs, arms, great guns, calf-muscle definition as good as Fish's friend Pit Bull (even hidden by the dress socks), NFL-neck. 265 pounds, Fish guessed. 250 minimum. Starting nose-guard thick almost everywhere. Not a nose-guard nose, though. His nose was very thin, this long strangely thin nose turned upward at the end and his pointed close-to-Vulcan ears were tufted with wiry brown hairs, angling away from the sky when he shuffled backward to practice a lob return. He wore an earring, too, a gold hoop like Fish's but not as simple. With more to it, somehow, but at this distance Jon couldn't tell what.

Jon was intrigued. His creative juices flowed and he studied A-boy more closely. A's really, truly thick fingernails were creamy and off-colored like clean ivory. His heavy fingers continuously locked and unlocked on the over-wrapped Selkirk paddle handle. He had small, deep-set eyes, far back along that long, thin nose. His eyebrows and his leg hair looked like his ear tufts, curly and wild and a true black. His brown skin was patchy and mottled, like Fish's mom's, but she had dyschromia, a common older-folk issue that mottles skin red and brown and purple like a royal tapestry. Fish didn't know what Aardvark had; he'd never seen the condition in a younger man.

Fish mused. Calling Aardvark 'young' meant only he was saying he was younger than Fish's mom. He didn't know Aardvark's age, but he had to be at least fifty, since he was playing in a senior tournament. It was obvious at a glance that the A was aware of the dangers of the desert sun on his skin. He had thick white zinc ointment slathered across his broad cheeks and what Fish swore was a Patagonia Longbill cap that shaded his face completely at certain angles. With a start, Fish recognized similarities; he also owned a Patagonia Longbill cap and also used lots of zinc!

Flash-flash, and Aardvark and Fish were suddenly playing doubles together, each dressed the same, Aardvark in Fish's monochromatic shorts and shirt and Fish wearing a robe, each of them slathered with the zinc, wearing the Patagonia Longbills, Mutt and Jeff out there but dressed the same; you hit 'em high, I'll hit 'em low.

Aardvark's sunglasses capped the look. Fish had to study these a bit to figure them out and realized they were actually olive flip-ups forced onto curved protective eye-guards like the ones Fish had used playing racquetball and squash years before. Except these eye-guards were safety yellow, more like pale yellow Home Depot safety glasses, with the green-brown flip-ups clipped on top. Fish blinked. No matter what, he would never flash on wearing those crazy glasses, but he did flash on wearing the pop-out slinky-eyes instead that people sproing at you during Halloween. Very cool, he decided. He'd have to get some for Halloween, just because.

When Fish moved past the A's outfit, he realized that while a regular human-type man, (albeit an unusual-looking one), Aard looked closer to an animal than any player he'd ever seen, irrespective of their nicknames. To be sure, his Arizona friends Pit Bull and Bear looked like … well, at least something like … a Pit Bull and a Bear, respectively. And Fish still really couldn't remember what an aardvark looked like anyway; he thought again that maybe his own mental image was more an anteater or more an aRRRR-madilo, mentally doing "Talk Like a Pirate." Flash … *a horse walked into a pirate bar. 'Ha-RRRR, matey,' called the bartender. 'Why the long face?'* Fish smiled at his stupid sense of humor. He loved that about himself.

Fish knew very well that appearances can be deceiving with pickleball players. They can have all the mechanical chops, the groundstrokes, the drops, the whole megillah, and still stink. Or the opposite. Or both on the same day. *Maybe he's good*, he thought. But no, not so much. The Aardvark looked weird but played much worse. *Beginner!* Fish thought at first, but quickly changed his mind. A-Dawg was far worse than that. The Aardvark was playing in the second-lowest skill bracket that offered singles, and he was so bad that Fish flashed: maybe the Aard hadn't ever seen singles played before? Maybe he was here 'cuz he lost a bet? In theory that could explain the outfit, too, of course; that was part of the bet? Fish examined the thought quickly and stored it for future exploration.

Having gone this far, now he analyzed the A's game. Fish had trained himself to have good observation skills but it ended there. He wasn't all that analytical by nature, but he did it very well, step by step, a skill he developed while learning project management at Bend Parks. A-vark was playing left-handed, like Jon, but unlike Jon, he didn't try to hit a deep serve. He couldn't hit a deep return. He displayed no power, no placement, nor any spin. He displayed neither dink, nor lob, smash, or drive. His stroke mechanics looking weak, he had neither forehand or backhand; he could only root around after balls, swatting at them as if creating a breeze, as if making actual contact wasn't really part of his plan. No way Fish could conjure up enough positive thoughts about his game to make a silk purse out of this Aardvark. Fish smiled to himself. He himself wasn't yet a pickleball winner in either double or in singles, but Aardvark was a straight-up singles loser who also looked like he was okay being a loser. At least it was different.

During the warm-ups the A did hit the ball sporadically; the odds almost guaranteed it. But when he did, nothing good happened. He hit out, hit long, or into the net. And any ball he hit into the opposing court was a floater, a sitter, a shiny-yellow multi-holed peach hanging there in no-man's land, ripe fruit waiting to be picked and eaten by his hungry opponent. Fish could have put most of those away himself and he was basically only a beginner. Maybe, he flashed, he could play the game from here in his seat, and at heart always a comic-book fan, imagined Eel O'Brian, Plastic Man from the old DC Comics, stretching to hit shots way over on Court One, and then saw himself married suddenly to Elasti-Girl and started thinking about their sex life, which made him nearly blow bile through his nose trying to stop his chortling. *'How big IS that thing, Eel?' 'Well, how big do you WANT it, baby?'* Good stuff!

The practice ended, Aardvark tossed his robe on the top of the fence in the back and the match began. Right off Fish noticed something beyond unique appearance and tragic play. Way beyond. Initially he thought it was his screwed-up left eye playing tricks, but when he put his hand over the bad eye he saw that, sometimes, not all the time, there was this — Fish didn't know — something about the A. Or around him, maybe. Fish was very reluctant to say the word out loud, but he thought it, okay, *an aura*. Even at best not visible, really, but never invisible, either. In a bizarre mental aside, Fish thought of peering at details on his laptop after his young boxer, Ray, had been licking its screen.

And this thing, this aura — whatever — it was possible it was real. When he looked at the A he saw blurs along the Aardvark's outline, as if he was watching through a smudged filter. Fish saw the aura and then didn't see it; it came and went, inconsistent. What remained constant was attitude. He was the most constant character Fish had ever seen on any court. And it was a positive consistency, not always grumpy like the Bear or perpetually ferocious like Pit Bull.

It took Fish a bit to figure it out, but at its root, it was fun-loving. It was a fun-loving attitude Aardvark showed in his whole being. His wide smile displayed long front yellowish teeth and set off his little olive-like eyes. His snorting, grunting laughter escaped after every shot, his steady unforced geniality was visible even in the face of his never actually scoring a point.

And there was more. His warmth extended to his opponent, even his laughter, now gathering him into his muscular furred arms at the end of their match, whispering something into the opponent's ear, something that made the man grin, nod his head, and punch the Aardvark lightly on the overstuffed shoulder, a kind of 'I hear that! Let's have a beer later!' kind of punch.

Fish wondered what he said. He knew it really didn't matter; the Aardvark was an extreme character in a young sport already known for its off-the-wall characters. And he lost with something more than grace, more like delight, or satisfaction. How could that be?

But the Aardvark was now out of this tournament, losing the match 15-0. Not much consolation for him left in this consolation round.

For some reason, Fish thought maybe the A-vark was worth meeting. That part was simple in pickleball. In this oddly friendly sport meeting folks was easy, everybody talked to everybody, so Fish went up to him, still on the court after his second match, now adjusting his robe.

"Hi," he said. "I'm Jon Fisher. Or just Fish. I watched you play. And I was wondering if I could ask you a question."

"I'm the Aardvark. Or just Aardvark." One corner of the shorter man's full dark lip turned up. Fish thought he was smiling but couldn't be sure.

"I like the way you watched me," Aardvark added, smiling for real but staring at Fish's feet. "You stayed almost present throughout!" he said. "Also," said the A, "you have wonderful shoes! I didn't realize K-Swiss even made the Lozan Lii's in men's sizes! What are those, 15s?"

Holy shit! When had the Aardvark had time to be observing Fish? Plus … coincidences accumulating … the reference to being present indicated he probably knew something about Buddhism, and he also knew about weird one-off court shoes. But that he even knew their size? That he also wore a Patagonia Longbill hat and zinc face cream? That he also had a gold earring, a hoop? That they were both left-handed? Too weird, like deja vu all over again. Maybe they would form a club! "Well, 14s, but yeah. Thanks, I guess," he said, but inside he was very pleased.

Buddhism only factored in Fish's life to the extent that he thought maybe he could get over feeling like throwing up when he lost, could gain some clarity and calm. Not that he adopted it for pickleball, but thinking about it for his pickleball game, sometimes he could see that pickleball was … well … not a metaphor for life. It was just pickleball. And when he had that perspective he played very well, like the descriptions of being in the zone but more conscious. He had read it once, 'To meet or realize self-love, lose disgust with yourself.' This again was classic Noel White, his favorite philosopher, but was that perfect? No, but it was close. The Aardvark was certainly a role-model for this behavior.

Plus, the A's approach to losing was light-years different than anything he had seen before. Fish was struck almost like a blow with a sudden thought. The A had lost badly and if he cared about that at all, Fish was a flounder. Was that the answer? Just not caring? Would that heal his reactions to losing? Well, of course it would, he thought, that was self-evident, but it was still losing.

While Fish was sizing up Aard and thinking profound thoughts, the Aardvark was also looking Fish over, moving up from feet to face, his furry eyebrows bunched a bit as he squinted at the Fish-man, horny hand up blocking the sun behind Fish's head. The Fish had seldom been on the receiving end of such a focused gaze, well, not since his dad had caught him in the act of stealing a dollar from his wallet in fifth grade. Six or ten seconds or a minute went by.

At last the A nodded briefly once, seemingly satisfied with something he saw. "You're thinking of my play and asking, 'Why,' I can see that easily enough," he said. "But that's not really your question, is it?"

At his words a new feeling came over Fish. Not bad. In fact, strange, but good. A warmth. His post-retirement nerves and ever-present hum of anxiety gone entirely. His jitteriness from before left as well. He could now feel his own breath as a balm, collecting deep in his chest, altogether the deepest calm he had felt in quite a while, maybe since actually getting his taxes done on time in early April last year. Somebody could see him, all of him.

*You're right!* thought Fish. It didn't matter, nothing mattered that had been wrong, like accounts of going to the light where the dying were shown their past sins and those sins don't matter because the provider of the light also showed them they were okay anyway, all was okay. Fish was okay. He hadn't been okay, and now he was. He had been on edge, nervous, now he wasn't. He connected with the Aardvark and melted into him, hearing again only that part of the sentence. "Not the question," Fish repeated to himself.

The other player and the referee had left the court. The Aardvark and Fish were alone. Fish looked down at him. Up close his tiny eyes were hooded, the veins of his short neck, red and pulsing with effort only minutes before, had disappeared into the mottled patches of his brown skin. His thick hands were locked on the handle of his red Selkirk paddle. He seemed at rest.

"I mean, maybe you're right. About my real question, anyway. How can anyone play so ... amazingly?"

"You mean ... play that badly? LOSE that badly?" The Aardvark smiled and lifted his thick eyebrows, just a question, no offense taken. "You can say it."

"Well ... yeah," Fish nodded. "Almost like you didn't care."

A beat while Aardvark thought about it. "Did you think all that might simply be Right Intention?" he smiled toothily, his voice like a snarky grunt, a phlegm-filled cough. He shrugged his robe back into place.

"I don't get you," Fish said. "What's your intention have to do with it?" Looking at the Aard up close was crazy-making, like looking too closely at a one-thousand-piece earth-toned jigsaw puzzle without benefit of a cover picture to guide him.

"Right Intention." Aardvark answered. "Right Intention takes work," he added, almost an afterthought. "Not caring about outcomes takes work."

"So ... intention takes work?" Fish asked.

"You really don't listen well, do you? RIGHT intention, grasshoppah." He tapped Fish's 'breathe' neck medallion hard with one horned fingernail. He traced around the infinity sign. "It's part of my practice, yes?" He stared up into Fish's eyes a foot above him, looking for some kind of answer. His strange deep-black eyes reminded the imaginative Fish of a black glass marble floating in blood-webbed egg whites. "If I can ask you a question now, what are you working on?"

Aardvark apparently didn't expect or need an immediate response, 'cuz he nodded politely to Fish and gathering his stuff, turned to leave. Fish watched his back walking away toward the court gate. He wondered if Aardvark was deaf, since neither 'intention' nor 'practice' seemed to answer any question he had asked.

Fish fingered his two-faced medallion, both the infinity sign and the Christian cross. It seemed warmer to the touch now, but that was impossible. Fish supposed he might never see the Aard again. For all he knew the Aardvark would never play pickleball again. Really, he had barely played this time. Fish smiled at the thought. And suddenly he felt a real urgency to ask him one question before the chance was gone.

The Aard was opening the gate now and a flash. An entirely different question floated into Fish's mind, rising as if in a magic-answer eight ball. "Do you play doubles?" Fish called. "Could we play sometime?"

Aardvark held the gate open, half-turning. "I do play doubles," he said. "And," pausing a bit theatrically, pointing in the air with his available hand, "maybe even more amazingly than singles!" Definitely a smile in his voice. "So, yes, maybe we should. Maybe we can even walk some of the Middle Path together! Call Dr. Sam. Then call me." He pulled the back of his robe around and pointed at the infinity sign or the Mobius strip or whatever it was on the robe's back and raised his eyebrows to signify ... something. "If I'm right, you might be a part of my solution!"

Then he left, closing the gate carefully behind him.

Fish just stood there. Part of what solution? And to what problem? Not to mention, the Aardvark knew Dr. Sam? Putting small-world blah-blah-blah aside, what would be the odds of that? More important, how did A-man know enough about Fish to tell him to call Sam to begin with? Unless, of course, it was the Aardvark who Sam had called from Bend. Why on earth would Sam want Fish to meet the Aardvark?

That last was strange beyond all imagining, Sam thinking about the Aardvark as Fish's next life coach. Flash — Jon was transported to a dusty plane, just he and Aardvark, Jon with both eyes covered, Aardvark leading him toward the edge of a cliff. Classic Fish thought. Blind leading the blind.

Least of all the questions was, 'Why should Fish call Sam about his playing doubles with Aardvark?' Too many questions and no answers at all.

## Chapter Eight

FISH DIDN'T LIKE MYSTERIES wrapped in enigmas, so for the moment he went to his fallback plan. He went about his business, which meant finishing this tournament with Jeff. And he — they — did finish. In fact, they did better than they had hoped. That one moment of profound clarity had disappeared; Fish knew that no feeling is permanent, but overall it had calmed him. He played relaxed, which in turn helped his partner. They stopped making so many unforced errors. Fish even stopped missing so many serves.

A week before he wouldn't have believed this possible, but now it was history, told, in truth ... in one game Fish successfully completed three drop shots on the same point, working his way to the line, a new best-in-class for him. He could even visualize each shot before it happened, like visualizing a golf shot swing out on the fairway, the ball landing within feet of the flag. True, they lost that point, but his approach was awesome.

Overall, Jeff and Fish dramatically improved from their starting point. They won their next 15-point consolation match, a different kind of blow-out, giving a near-donut to two nice but outclassed guys snow-birding in from Iowa.

The next game was hard-scrabble and hard fought to the end. Sometimes a score doesn't say much about the game. Early though this was in his pickleball career, he had already found you could play a game and win it 11-2 and you knew, and the other team knew, that it was just the breaks. That it could go back and forth and change from game to game. Or one person, usually Jon, lost his serve. Or if it was your day, you hit the top of the tape three times and all three balls dropped into the opponents' kitchen. Or you hit an out-ball and the wind blew it back in. All that was a very real part of pickleball. It wasn't just the old NFL bullshit — on any given Sunday. It was maybe like that a little, but not much.

True, some teams should never beat him, and early in his development, he never should have beat some other teams. Never ever. But still, there were those variables, and often they ultimately decided a match. Like Karma really was a real-live bitch, not merely a concept. Here, in this game, no variables influenced the match, not really. It was close all the way and either team could have won. Both teams played pretty darn well, made lots of shots. Typical for pickleball, there might be mini-runs of two or three points, but they were rare, maybe one on each side. There were lots of side-outs with no points scored. Because it was a consolation game they switched sides at eight points, but the score was close. They were still 8-7, and stayed there within a point of each other, back and forth, everyone in the game, way in the game, in the zone, really. Jeff, who had previously lost, then regained his own serve in the preceding match, rocked, made great gets, got everything over the net, like a middle-aged superstar.

Three things happened, all positive, that were each very unexpected and contributed to Jeff and Fish's win.

At 15-15, opponents' second serve, the right court opponent popped up a sitter that anyone could have put away and Fish did, hammering it like Pit Bull, bending it like Beckham, a power shot using all his leverage, perfectly timed but into the middle of the net. In his past lives, not so long ago, the disgust would have kicked in and Fish would be ruminating about his inadequacies for two shots into the future, making it impossible for them to climb past his unforced error.

This time, though, he recognized the flash of anger that washed through him like a burning wave; he saw it as an old friend, and then he saw himself. He flashed on the anger flowing through him and wanted it gone, not sticking around. He stuck his paddle up and called their first time-out.

At 15-15 again, this time Fish on first serve, right court, he got caught coming too far into the middle and his opponent, a cagey white-bearded character nicknamed SW, or Swiss Watch for the precision of his placement, cut the ball across him, with the ball hitting in but jumping rapidly toward the sideline and then outside of it. Acting intuitively, never having tried the shot before, Fish slid outside with the ball, let it continue out, and far outside the net post, changed hands, and with his right hand simply tapped the ball back into the opponent's court, just behind SW's left foot. A changing-hands-around-the net-post-shot, no thought of it being a foot-fault, perfect execution, resulting in a one-point advantage.

16-15 now and SW smacked a solid service return down the alley past Fish's backhand, and the second serve passed to his partner, Jeff. Fish held up a hand and took their final timeout. "Let's stay cool," he said. "We only need the one point. Let's just keep it in play." When play resumed, Jeff hit a very conservative serve, two-thirds back, trying only to keep it in play, sticking to the game plan. And they did win it, the longest point of the longest match for sure. Both teams waited it out, mostly content with just dinking ahead and center-net-dink and cross-court-dink and repeat, maybe dozens of times, not very inspired shots, really, but keeping the ball in play until finally Swiss-Watch pulled the trigger, ripping it cross-body at Fish, who almost did a face-plant getting out of the way, and the ball went long. Comical move, worked perfectly. What a concept, patience.

With that win they were two off the bubble for medaling in the maxed-out bracket, but next lost (and appropriately, Fish thought) to the same team that had beaten them in the first round in two fairly close games, these being Chance and Flynn, a team of sandbaggers, really, guys more than qualified to go up to 4.5 and who had nonetheless and inexplicably found a way to lose once in the top bracket. Chance had a serve like a cannon, and Flynn could literally get anything back softly and properly, considered his defense to be his offense and proved it. Fish and Jeff played even with them, too, for a few points, anyway, a respectable final of 15-9 at the end, and a nod of approval from each of the two opponents when they tapped paddles at the net.

All things considered, Fish thought, this was really a satisfactory performance, winning two matches, coming within telescopic range of a medal, losing (twice) but only to the team that eventually took gold. But strangely he didn't see it as an accomplishment at all. It wasn't a non-accomplishment, either. Accomplishment didn't have anything to do with it. In his mind he liked the idea of a medal, and the ones they gave at Palm Creek looked colorful and heavy and nice, but in a theoretical way, like a person might enjoy a colorful painting in a museum. He could enjoy it without being attached to the idea of owning it. Something inside of him had shifted, almost seismically.

Fish went back early to his tidy motor home. This also was not like him, him the newbie, the one who hung around usually until the last dog is hung but he did have dog-duty, speaking of dogs. He brought out Ray, his 14-month-old Brindle boxer pup, advised him to pee and poop and stretched him a bit with a brief jog to the big southern dog park.

Ray, lucky dog, was there in time to rough-play awhile with Ruby, a remarkably beautiful fawn female boxer, and with Zack the black lab, all young dogs, doing what young dogs do, getting small with each other, jowling at each other, showing off the top of their still-maturing back-of-the-throat voices, rolling in the grass. Sitting on the dog park bench with Gene and Margaret, Ruby's owners, and with the other dog owners was pleasant. Fish enjoyed watching their dogs bark ferociously and roll on each other, but thoughts of Sam kept intruding. *I'll have to call, maybe tomorrow,* he thought.

Fish was surprised to find that some of the other dog-folks had seen him at the tournament. To his pleasure, he found they liked what they had seen in the later matches. Fish wasn't used to compliments on his pickleball play and he grinned and hung around, preening a bit, acting disappointed that he hadn't got into the medal rounds, but happy and modest about how well they had done. Sitting there in the evening cool, his arms draped over the bench, watching his dog play hard and wrestle, this was very good, Fish thought. A very good day. Thoughts of the Aardvark faded away a little, not like they were going anywhere, but not staying front-of-mind, passing through the way thoughts do.

Back at the coach, Fish wiped the grass and mud off Ray's paws, popped the top off a Corona, sat with his dog on their dark-brown couch, pulled up the big TV from the center console, turned on a previously taped fly fishing show and day-dreamed a little more about the Aardvark, just a thought, something about pack and family, although later he thought there might have been another word used.

His thoughts were drowned out by televised calls of "There's One!" and "Fish On!" Ray kept nuzzling closer, finally resting his jowls on Fish's lap, snoring, snurfling, belching, and farting like any healthy boxer. Fly fishing was sometimes better than pickleball in a way, Fish thought. It didn't have winners and losers. Fish suspected that Ray, being a dog, always thought his owner was a winner. He thought the same about Ray, that good dog.

Later, thinking of Sam, Fish made a little stir-fry with riced cauliflower and onions and chopped chicken livers and thigh meat and spooned a bit into Ray's dish to mix with the drooling pup's food. This was a mistake, of course, but one that goes with owning a boxer, and he didn't hold the bilious farts against the pretty boy-dog at all.

He did his stretches and his before-bed rituals, which included his evening prayers to Christ Jesus, his main squeeze. Siddhartha Gautama was the historical Buddha but otherwise not so important to Fish. Certainly Gautama had never considered himself even a lower-case god, and Fish didn't either and didn't pray to him.

But tonight he added something different for Christ Jesus to think about. For his daily special, as he called it. Tonight he asked Jesus to keep Aardvark safe. And maybe to bring them together sometime, maybe play a little pickle. But not until he called Sam, of course, and got a clean bill of health from Sam about the Aard. He climbed into the coach's air bed, then got right out and found the card Sam had given him and stared at it. It could be an aardvark, sure enough. An exploding aardvark? Flash! But what had he flashed on? What good was intuition or creativity if you couldn't remember what you had intuited or created? He climbed back in and slept all night, straight through.

# Chapter Nine

IN THE MORNING, Fish began the dance by calling Sarah at Sam's office, complimenting her for her great voice and promptness in answering and being sure to impress upon her how important it was that Sam call soon. He told Sarah to write down the word aardvark, if for no other reason than to see if that attracted Dr. Sam's attention.

It worked, but only somewhat. Dr. Sam called back and left a message, but it was well past the end of a long day when Fish was already in bed. Sam's message was longer than his usual but still a bit cryptic. "So you met Aardvark," his message said. "Aardvark's the real deal. David went to school with him at Boston College. Can you even imagine?" Sam laughed out loud as he said that, as if he were the funniest man alive, thinking that his middle son, David, who had initially gone into one of the nation's best theology and comparative religion programs, one Fish himself had looked into for five minutes once, would somehow be a friend with this Aardvark.

Over the next couple of days, Fish tried a few more times but never made live contact with Sam, and so, just to have closure, decided to 'friend' the Aard in the social media of his mind and let the whole thing go, if only for now.

During his last few days at Palm Creek, Fish took care of some business. The first was strictly personal. After the tournament he had gotten to know Joan, the sixty-ish woman he had sat next to and shared pushes with at the tournament, and found she was not prim at all. Not even a tiny bit, in fact. If the RV's rockin', don't come a-knockin', as the saying goes. They had had a great time together and he realized how little time he had made for women in his life since the divorce. It felt like an opportunity he had lost, then suddenly found. A good thing, he thought.

But Joan already had plans that didn't include him. Their goodbyes were sweet and included promises to stay in touch, to see ya down the road, keep the rubber side down, and all that. He had a twinge or two as she pulled out, one of the independent women he was beginning to realize were out here in pickleball world, the ones driving their own RVs. Joan drove a nifty little Mercedes-powered front-engined Euro-styled rig. An RV-ing woman without a man was like Fish without his bicycle, he thought, laughing aloud at his own stupid Gloria Steinham pun and waving at her as she turned her gleaming silver and burgundy rig down Palm Creek Drive toward the open road. He felt pretty good about her, and about himself, for that matter.

With the tournament over, he stuck around longer and played a little more ball with a few of the big boys on the challenge courts where they couldn't say no. After play, he exercised Ray a bit and then checked out the tournament schedule site pickleballtournaments.com and the tournament list on USAPA.org evenings in his rig. Slowly he identified a few tournaments he'd like to play in. The disabilities he felt — his left eyesight, his inexperience, and his performance anxiety or losing phobia — he decided to keep trying to overcome. He didn't want to treat pickleball as a life and death sport, not really, but he did take it seriously, so he made a list of those folks he thought he could match up with as partners, not the absolute top tier of his age/skill group; people who might not be disappointed going two and out as long as they had played okay. He looked for both men and women.

During one evening's partner search, he realized that, like him, many of the folks registered with nicknames. They had their own avatars, names and images they adopted, that manifested a characteristic or an attribute or something they wanted to become or at least become known as. This was a little confusing as their 'new' name would appear on pickleballtournaments.com, but not on the USA Pickleball Association, or USAPA site, as if one was where people played, and the other more serious, like a repository of birth or death certificates or something.

He began thinking more about this one windy night, sitting on the couch killing time, as the gusts outside rocked his Winnebago. He picked up a yellow pad and started listing men and women he'd identified that he could play with, that in his own mind at least he matched up with, and who also had alter-ego style and names to match. They included Angel, Blue Steel, Boomer, Boz, The Captain, Captain Kirk, Champ, Coke, Cookie, Fidget-Ass, Flash, Fly Girl, Four-Star, Hillbilly, Hollywood, Ivy (and Poison Ivy), JR Mint, Killshot, Little Bus, Magnum, Marine, Mills, Mr. C., Mr. T, Mr. Z., Pork Chop, The Professor, Rocket, Rum (husband of Coke), "Black" Steele, Striker, Sugar Shane, SW (Swiss Watch), Tater, The Captain, T-Bone, The Chosen One, The Train, Wonder Woman, White Lightning, and Yoda, to name a few.

Another whole group of folks identified themselves from others having the same given name, the most common being "Tall" vs. "Small" … Tall Paul vs. Small Paul, Tall Bill vs. Small Bill. Sometimes there would be three the same, the record being a rural pickleball club where he found six Bobs: Big Bob, Good Bob, Bad Bob, and so on. He wondered how the names were awarded and by whom?

But the largest single category of names seemed to be

animals: Badger, Batgirl, Bear, Cat, Cheetah, Dog, El Condor, Fox, Nemo, Nole the Mole, Pit Bull, Rhino, Snake, Three-Dog, Two-Dog, Silver Fox. And he himself, he smiled. Fish. Not very imaginative, Fish. Worked for him, though. He flashed on a fish, fishing in a future fishy furnace. What? Still crazy after all these years, he thought. He smiled. Crazy wasn't all bad.

## Chapter Ten

A FEW DAYS LATER, barely April, Fish headed back to Bend to tie up loose ends. This, his first shakedown trip, had gone well thus far. His meditation sucked and (facing the truth) his life was still a bit messy, but so far, so good. And so, he decided, he and Ray were going on the road, this time for real.

But he had a house to close up or at least rent for a longer period, his parents to say goodbye to, a work sponsored going-away party for him at his parents' clubhouse up at Rocky Ridge. Fish, in and around Bend his whole life, unsatisfied this whole time with his family, his home, even his beautiful city, would soon be a full-timer or at least a snowbird, for real.

And, like everyone, he wanted what he couldn't have and grasped to have the solidity and good vibes he imagined he'd always had in Bend and now wouldn't have. False news, false memories; he tried to let all that fall through.

One evening toward dusk on the trip back, up North on Highway 5, they stopped in Red Bluff at a very nice RV park on the river. Ray sat in the passenger seat mooning at the pretty Australian shepherd in the next coach over while Fish sat in the middle of the floor practicing meditation.

Because he felt like it, Fish lit a candle on the top of the TV cabinet. It was a sandalwood-scented candle somebody had given him; he thought it was a girl, maybe

Joan. It had a pleasant herbal fragrance. The flame flickered steadily, a good solid wick, a nice candle for meditating.

He put the lit candle in front of the card Sam had given him. He followed his breath, focusing on the flame. Time began to drop away. He felt each breath, attended to two breaths without distraction, then three, then, at once, five. His mind/conscious/subconscious/ego/id/whatever ... who cares ... went into hyperdrive and flashed on Aardvark. This was maybe the best meditating he'd done, but he came up from it clear-headed to think about the Aardvark.

Watching the man from this perspective, without judgment, without any agenda, was interesting. He still couldn't understand why he'd had played the singles match the way he did. He wasn't sure but suspected for the first time that Aardvark could play the game very well indeed, if and when he chose to. Nothing Fish could have pointed to logically would have led to that conclusion, but he believed it as you believe the sun will come up in the East. It simply will, and that's a fact you can take to the bank.

He stayed with Aardvark through all of an imaginary match, watching him. He realized late into it that he, Fish, was now playing doubles with the Aard. And that it was just play, all good, SO much fun it felt like joy, light, all heaviness gone from his body.

He never saw his opponents, but saw the ball floating and revolving slowly, coming to him, showing its molded seams, saw his paddle making exact contact in the middle of the sweet spot. Feeling something like exultation, but without the excitement. Excitement was a shallow emotion. This was more than excitement.

When he awoke he was in bed and it was very late in the evening. He had, apparently, gone from meditating to feeding and walking Ray, who was snoring beneath his blanket on the couch, curled up like a cinnamon roll.

He looked around, saw that all was normal and accounted for, and didn't even bother getting up to check the lock, rolled over and went back to sleep.

## Chapter Eleven

TWO DAYS LATER Fish was in Bend, staying out on Highway 20 at the Bend-Sisters RV Park, which both he and Ray liked a lot. He had dinner with his parents, first night, who put on the dog a bit and showed off their new home, which was beautiful, on a bluff overlooking the Deschutes River with tons of glass everywhere and a tiered deck to die for. Ray met their miniature schnauzer, Molly, a new-to-them rescue and easily as playful as Ray, and the two dogs romped around the deck, making all three of their owners laugh and making Fish wonder if his parents cared that Ray was making nail marks in the Trek decking, and deciding that was their issue, so let it go.

Now that he was back in Bend he decided to give his RV some additional attention. While cheap money and good credit had helped him finance his lightly-used brown 36' Winnebago Journey with three television sets and more features than he had in his tiny but dated westside Bend house, his first shake-down run to Palm Creek had showed him a few things he wanted to tune up a bit.

Fish practiced connecting and disconnecting the black-water hoses three times more times, and then went for the gold and replaced a very sticky black water valve. He went underneath the coach on a dolly ... how else could somebody with his height move around under a coach ... tightened all the clamps, sprayed Rustoleum where it might need it, and sprayed the proper grease on various moving parts like the slides.

He moved inside the coach. He remembered a friend had had a closet clothes bar fall out of his fifth-wheel bumping down Highway 5, so he checked those and also tightened up all the cabinet hardware latches that were already loosening from their short time on the road.

Next, he thought about his own comfort, what his aging back would feel like after he subjected it to the equivalent of a continuous class-5 earthquake bouncing down the road every day as a full-time RVer. A couple of days later he wangled a service appointment at Large County RV to replace the driver's seat with an air-suspension seat. He winced paying the bill. "You'll be glad you did this," Lee Jr., the service manager, said. Lee Jr. was the captain's son and a good businessman as well as a good fisherman, and even a decent pickler in his own right. Someone Fish could trust.

"Right," Jon said. "At least as glad as you'll be with the bonus you'll get for making that sale! You guys didn't seem to remember I bought this clunker from you!"

"You kidding?" Lee Jr. asked, incredulous. "We don't even TRY to make money off used RV sales. We sell 'em to you guys at cost and catch up when you bring 'em in for service!"

They looked at each other, each trying to pretend anger, and both finally laughing, giving it up, both knowing that Lee Jr. told truth and that Fish knew all that going in.

Preparations continued. Fish got his own medical stuff done, updated Ray's shots, got a copy of Ray's medical records on CD to take with (boxers being known for coming down with more serious stuff involving gastric and heart systems, not just for their incessant sulfurous farting). As an afterthought he had all his own medical stuff put on a CD, too. Why should he treat his dog better than he treated himself?

Then he got a mailbox set up. Oregon isn't a bad state to

be from as a full-timer, but he needed postal service. Drew at Postal Connected down on Third was happy to help.

"How often will you forward mail?" Fish asked. "I'm a little concerned I'll miss something."

Drew looked at him sort of sadly, the way you look at anybody who is talking to you out of total ignorance but without maliciousness, the way you look, for instance, at a retarded young child.

"We'd be happy to forward mail every day for you," Drew said. "But if you're willing to take my advice here, I'd say just forward once a month. We'll throw away junk mail, fliers, and crap. Send you the rest. And I'll call you if they send a certified letter to tell you you've won the lottery or something. Deal?"

Agreeing to this seemed serious. He was entrusting another of his life-lines, his ability to access his own mail, to someone else. This was giving up more control in return for freedom to move around without caring. But how could he not care?

He took a breath and remembered waking up in the night what seemed like a year ago, all the things he was trying to control swirling around in his mind. It was then he simply said, "Right. We'll go for a month." And now here he was, signing his rights away to his own mail. "Just don't screw up when that lottery ticket does come," he finished.

"What lottery ticket?" asked Drew, blandly.

## Chapter Twelve

WHILE IN BEND Fish took Ray for several fun outings, up to the various high-country lakes that were opening early after the mild winter they'd had. East Lake was open, Paulina, Hosmer, Crane Prairie. He bought what he concluded was the world's best single person with dog and RV inflatable fishing boat, a beautiful little number from ScoutInflatables.com called the Scout365.

This well-thought-out little gem was inflatable in a matter of seconds, had a hard bottom Fish could insert, had a lean bar, and could be used with his electric trolling motor. Ray initially hated boating but by the end of their second outing on Big Lava, Ray had his front haunches completely up on the front pontoon and his muzzle almost entirely in the water, helping Fish land a couple of Rainbows and (uncharacteristic for the lake) a good-sized Brook trout, all of which Fish carefully released to the bewilderment of his dog.

A little more work on his boat and he had wheels on it, could easily disassemble it and store it in the single bay underneath his coach that (through the miracle of good engineering) was a complete pull-out bay on either side. Now he was mobile and agile. Flash ... an image of him playing pickleball with one hand, out of the boat, steering the boat's electric trolling motor with the other ... an entertaining enough image that Fish didn't worry too much about the logical disconnect.

Most dogs travel well when brought to it early and Ray was no exception, but some RV travel sounds made him nervous, especially when Jon's exhaust brake downshifted and made strange hold-me-back noises. The Cascades Lakes Loop that Fish drove on during their fishing trips was ideal for desensitizing Ray, having quick ups-and-downs that forced the rig to continuously shift into exhaust-brake mode.

Initially the exhaust brake noises caused Ray to respond in kind, and unfortunately for the consistency of Ray's training, Fish thought it was funny as hell when Ray would start to howl at the noise of the downshift in that way some dogs do at the sounds of sirens, his young but deep voice cracking and warbling here or there.

Fish knew he would not think it was funny at all if this went on for any length of time. So he donated a whole day to Ray's training, driving clear up off Highway 97 to Paulina and then back down again, downshifting at every corner, and turning around and doing it again, and then a third time. Finally, Ray had had enough and gave up the howling. Immersion therapy for boxers! Fish loved it.

After Ray had had some boat time and some non-howl time and was pretty much dialed in on the whole RV thing they went 'home' to the Bend-Sisters park for a couple of down-days. The little park featured a small lake where lots of nice trout cruised. Fish didn't fish for them, though he could have; fishing was allowed. But he felt it was too much like shooting fish in a barrel, flashing on him, in a barrel, and the park owner, Lydia, shooting at him. But while Ray didn't know whether to poop or go blind about the big trout before, now he just sat by the shore and stared at the big hybrid rainbows, occasionally looking up at Fish as if to say, "That big roller is gobbling nymphs! We could snag him, at least!" in a somewhat accusing sort of way.

There was one more thing he wanted to do about Ray. He

wanted to make sure that, if he needed to — say over a pickleball tournament weekend or such — he could find a kennel that would take him and treat him well. But first, Ray needed another step in his training.

Ray was a boxer. Boxers as a breed have a way of looking directly at you. And at other dogs. They aren't being aggressive when they do it, but most other breeds of dogs interpret a direct stare as aggressive. So sometimes dog fights occur and while boxers seldom will bite another dog, they are, in fact, boxers. They can hit with their front legs like kangaroos. Ray had hit Fish once or twice when they were rough-playing down on the floor and it hurt. A lot. So he contacted High Desert Veterinary, where Tony and the gang were, all who loved Ray almost as much as he did … if that were possible.

"CJ," he said when he called, "I've read about Good Citizen Training for dogs. Can Tony suggest where I could take Ray to get that?"

CJ had the answer. "Bend Pet Resort next door has a great program, Fish."

Perfect! Fish enrolled right away. In just a few short weeks Fish was displaying Ray's Good Citizen Certificate in the front window of his RV.

With the careful preparation completed, it wasn't that long before the dog was relaxed about the RV and even sat in the passenger seat on the way home, helping Fish navigate by staring intently at other cars and huffing occasionally at their dogs. Good dog!

Fish thought they were ready and hoped they could figure out whatever else needed to be figured out once they were on the road.

# Chapter Thirteen

WHEN IT CAME TO PICKLEBALL, Fish was all in. He was hooked and wanted to get better and compete more strongly. He had transferable skills to burn, he'd gone to college on that near-full-ride tennis scholarship, ranked second on his team by the time he'd been fired for choking on his serves. More recently he'd been Bend's open-division runner-up table tennis player two of the last five years. Fish had great eye-hand, fair mobility, decent knees. And of course, there was his height and a near-NBA wing-span measured in the day at 6' 8".

Pickleball was a different game from tennis or table-tennis, in some respects requiring more thinking, more of the analytical skills he didn't admit he had. But he had mad skills to start with. His eyesight was causing him some issues in the middle when he was in the right (deuce) court, but he thought with the right partner, maybe another lefty like himself, they could stack. Stacking is pickleball-speak for "arrange themselves so their respective strong-hands are both always in the middle." The aim of this formation is to avoid many of the unforced errors caused by an opponent hitting directly between them when their backhands were there and losing the point.

He was maybe unrealistic, but what difference did it make? It gave him something to be excited about, something to work on. He already knew he could never play competitively with the younger pros. They were like gazelles on steroids. They could get to anything, get any shot back, and playing against each other the rallies could last forever. Which is to say you simply didn't get to the medal rounds by accident. You got what you earned.

He knew that level was out of reach for him. But his ego told him that with his sports background and athleticism, with all his physical attributes combined with his one recent tournament result, surely he could play with the top amateurs, if not now, then soon. Or at least eventually. He was scoping out the competition regularly now and watching every tournament result online, determining who was moving up and who down.

He always kept an eye out for the Aardvark and sometimes, pretty often really, he saw results for him, mostly in the Western half of the U.S., not only the Southwest. The Aard played in California some and in Washington, once in Montana and twice in Idaho. Not in Oregon, not yet, but Fish thought he might get there. There was no pattern to where he would show up, not that Fish could see, anyway.

Relative to medal points, the A's results were slim. He was not winning tournament points, but he was winning more matches, always playing with a different partner, but in the 4.0 bracket he was moving up. Fish thought there were two interesting things there. First, that he could find partners, as it seems the word does get around about good or bad play. And second, his results were improving. Fish smiled at the memories of his own play and wondered what it would take to truly get himself headed in the right direction. Never, ever miss a serve. Master of the basics.

Ray and Fish kept moving. February came and went, then March. He was surprised how much he liked the desert; he enjoyed Arizona. But in April he went to New Mexico, spent time in Santa Fe. He played pickleball everywhere, and was moving up, playing with the best players who would have him during recreational play and medaling maybe 10 percent of the time at 4.0. He was also learning what he was missing in his game. It amounted to both mental and emotional stuff; focus and calm. No tennis match in collegiate competition had ever caused him this kind of stress. He supposed because he cared more now and identified with it. To his surprise, he was finding a new identity as a pickleball player. Not always that of a winner, but excepting the serve, someone who could get the job done.

Fish had to force himself to admit it once or twice but he could be pretty good. An outside observer would have said he had all the shots, even something of a soft game, even an irregular but improving corner drop shot from the baseline. In one tournament he surprised everyone — and himself — by hitting a match-winning drop from mid-court against a left-handed opponent at the line in the deuce court.

He sliced the ball cross-court to his opponent's backhand and back-spun the ball into the net. It was a pro-level shot that was way, way above Fish's 4.0 pay grade and it stunned his opponent, a solid older player who looked at it, looked up at Fish, tapped his paddle face, and mouthed "nice shot." That got Fish applause and he admit he loved it, hitting a show-stopper when he needed it most and winning to boot. Shallow thing that he was.

'Course he couldn't do that all the time and as often as not his nerves got to him and he'd commit really terrible unforced errors, just 'cuz of losing his calm and focus. His zazen practice helped a little bit: he would go into 'hiding' before a medal match and follow his breath down as far as he could. Meditation for him was still something he sucked at, but every little bit helped. But then there were times he would play too hard, or not hard enough, or concentrate too hard or not enough, and make unforced errors by the bushel, and he hated that in himself. He was able, physically able, to play at a high level, he thought. He certainly had done so in tennis, although he was clear with himself tennis is a different game with what he thought was a simpler playing strategy then competitive pickleball.

Certainly, pickleball was important to Fish now. He wouldn't go to a city that didn't have it available. But it wasn't everything. He didn't forget about Ray, or about fishing, or about his practice. Ray and Fish ran more now, sometimes only half an hour, sometimes three times that. Being a young boxer with a typical boxer's smooshed-in face, Ray's bred-in breathing issues meant he over-heated easily. But they'd go out early, get to some nice packed dirt trail so the dog's pads wouldn't get worn — besides everything else, boxers have proportionately tiny feet and their pads get mightily messed up — and Fish would rest if dog-breath needed it or asked for water by nosing the bottle Fish carried, and gradually they both got in much better condition.

Fish knew they were both finally in good form when one day they got out at 6 a.m., just before full light, and ran 90 minutes outside Tucson in the foothills without stopping, Ray's giant tongue lolling about but not in a bad way, a happy grin on his face. He knew he was earning his breakfast. In fact, Ray was eating like a horse but still keeping his weight off. Always wiry, Fish was leaner than he had ever been, dropping under two bills and staying there. And his new and improved conditioning often came in very handy late in a tournament, especially when coming up through the loser bracket. Going the long way, his partner-de-jour and he would have to play virtually everybody else in the bracket and then win twice in the final if they were to take gold, which he hadn't yet done.

Fishing was off again, on again. Not everywhere in the West is trout-friendly. It certainly depended on where they were. Idaho, Montana, Wyoming ... marvelous. Colorado, okay, great in places. California, not wonderful, with exceptions like Fall River, the Trinity, Upper Sac, the McCloud. Arizona, generally poor, except Lee's Ferry on the Colorado. These were all opinions, he knew, and others' mileage may vary, but he didn't try to go everywhere, and this is what he found where he did go. Since he only fly-fished, not all places were created equal for his preferred style of fishing, either.

Perhaps the best outing he and Ray had was at the Green River in Utah on the way back to Bend in early May. He fished early with a guide in his Dory, Ray standing chest-out in the bow, hogging the best spot but having a great time, his tiny boxer tail wagging for no reason, drippy jowls pulled back in a grin and creating puddles. Even fishing second position behind Ray, using a fast 5-wt rod and tiny flies, Fish was doing great. Fishing was outstanding for hot fish on dry flies and tiny Callibaetis nymphs, biggest trout about 22". He'd caught many bigger in Bend, but this one was truly feisty on a little #20 barbless hook.

Meditation-wise, he continued as best he could. He was sitting zazen, meditating and following breath, maybe five or six days a week now, up to maybe an hour's duration. He continued to read (and watch YouTube) to learn more about Buddhism. And although he had no teacher, he felt he was making progress in his understanding of this very ... is 'complex' the right word? ... religion. (He wondered, too, is 'religion' the right word?)

He loved what he was reading even though he couldn't put the pieces together. The three of this. The eight of that. Buddhism uses numbers like some people use board puzzles, putting the pieces in front of you and letting you put them together, and for Fish they didn't always fit. But what he liked about it was how it instructed him to lead a useful and calm life. He remembered how important 'calm' was last year when he felt so completely out of control. Now was better, glimpses of something deeper, that one weird experience outside Red Bluff, almost like a vision, that one, but Fish was still looking for a consistent supply of calm. Fish didn't think of himself as a Buddhist. When he thought of it at all, he thought he'd never be a Buddhist. Maybe an Episcopalian. Another question mark in his mind.

It was turning colder. Ray and Fish had been on the road for a few months. During the summer Mom called, announced that she and Dad were celebrating their fifty-seven years together on a cruise into both the Western and Eastern Mediterranean with a few days more on the ground on all sides of the cruises, exploring areas they had always talked about. They'd be out a month or so, wouldn't be around for Fish to help them celebrate their anniversary. They would be fine, they said, but somehow it made him a bit lonely, like maybe he didn't matter to them (a thought he put aside as rubbish a bit later), but also took away the bungees that would otherwise spring him and Ray back to Bend earlier.

At night he would cozy up, usually on the couch with Ray, and scroll through news until it peaked his anxiety, and then through tournament results which calmed him again. The Aardvark was still playing the tournaments fairly regularly. But now the world had shifted on its axis. The world's worst player had won a medal, Silver, in the heavily populated 4.0 bracket at a very competitive tournament in Southern California. Was it an accident?

He studied the bracket results more closely. No, no forfeits that advanced him, no weak bracket sides that Aardvark could exploit. Most were good, solid players Fish knew or knew of, folks who knew the complete game, both soft game and hard game, and could execute either on demand, although not with the same consistency and success as in the higher levels. Fish didn't know what to make of him having won a medal, the picture in his mind of Aardvark playing so poorly in Casa Grande was still that strong.

Fish traveled on and then on again, and then, to his surprise, the Aard medaled again at 4.0. Fish himself had recently and unexpectedly medaled at Huntsman in St. George with his friend and now occasional partner Pit Bull, and he thought how ironic it was that the worst player in the world had moved up at about the same pace. Fish thought about him, but then took no action beyond that. He had his own path, and Ray and he were out and about, seeing what other life there was beyond Bend. But not wanting to lose whatever small connection they had made, he sat down and clicked through on the 'find a player' feature on the USAPA.org site, found Aardvark Rinpoche, Aardvark listed as his only first name, and sent him a message.

*Hello, Aardvark. You might remember I talked to you in Palm Creek last March? And we said we might play doubles together sometime. Should we try and set a date? Maybe a tournament in Bend, Oregon. I'll be in Oregon quite a bit this summer. Congrats on the medals at 4.0, by the way. I got one at Huntsman, too.*

*Fish*

Fish didn't expect to hear anything all that soon. He thought, he didn't know why, that the Aardvark was maybe not the kind of guy to monitor his email all the time. And, of course, he couldn't call him, as his telephone number, assuming he had one, wasn't listed. So it was nice that he heard the next day.

*Good morning, Jon. I do indeed remember you, and especially your shoes. I would enjoy playing with you. Will you be in the Pacific Northwest in the summer? I would be happy to play a tournament with you in Bend. No Pressure. Just for the experience, you understand. Another step on the path!*

*Aardvark*

Hmmm … Jon didn't know what to make of the last half of the remark. Plus, he thought the Bend tournament might be full at the 4.0 level. But there was always the little Sunriver tournament, a funky who-cares little tournament, the first pickleball tournament in Central Oregon, about twelve years old if Fish remembered correctly. A beautiful setting, the Thousand Trails RV park, set right on the Little Deschutes River, all very low-key, a tournament in Central Oregon which happened before the Pickleball Zone Pacific Northwest Regional USAPA Championships.

Jon wrote to Aardvark, saying the same, that the Pickleball Zone was probably full. To his surprise, once again the Aard got back to him promptly and with more agreement than he expected.

*"Agree with you about Sunriver,"* Aard's message said. *"But can we try for Bend, too? Anne knows both of us. Maybe she'll help out. Also, forgot to ask again. What are you working on these days?"*

Fish stared at the message. In for a penny, he thought. Fish checked online; the 4.0 was full. He paid his fee anyway, put both himself and the Aardvark on a wait list and called Anne, the tournament director. He had been friendly with Cheetah for a couple of years now and she'd been known to help her friends when she could.

Writing back, he said,

*Hi, Aardvark. Bend is full but we're on the wait-list. You'll have to register to confirm we're willing to play. I'm checking in with Anne, too. So let's keep our fingers crossed. By the way, what did you mean when you asked me what I was working on?"*

Jon ended by giving his telephone number so they could move beyond online messaging. Sure as Satan, he quickly got a text, showing an icon of a 'real' aardvark as his avatar.

*Meant 'what are you working on personally.' Did you think I meant pickleball?*

The text from Aardvark ended with a smiling emoticon with two stick figures and what looked, for all intents and purposes, like a tiny, hand-drawn series of little shock-waves or lightning bolts or something.

Jon didn't know how to answer that, other than to think, *I wonder if he's been talking to Sam?* And what does it all mean?

## Chapter Fourteen

IT WAS EARLY JULY, a week before the Thousand Trails tournament. Fish pulled in and got his assigned spot, one he had asked for back in the woods maybe 100 yards west of the far restroom. Thousand Trails is a private campground but caters to families as much as anything, and Jon liked kids, or the idea of kids, but he didn't like parking next to them. Too damned noisy and Ray, for reasons the dog had, so far kept to himself, loved to howl at the sound of a dozen loopy kids riding Razors back and forth on the hard-packed dirt-and-gravel roads.

Fish thought Ray was hilarious when he howled, as the young dog would start with some kind of fruity warble, look at Fish like he knew he was gonna catch it now, and then, if Fish didn't discourage him, would get increasingly full-voiced as if he were practicing and finding his range. But Fish was also aware that not all neighbors felt that great about his boxer's howling, and he wanted to accord to them the same courtesy he asked of them ... keep it down.

Anyway, for his own reasons he had nailed down one of the most remote spots, and although it took him a full six or seven minutes to stroll down to the pickleball courts from there, that gave him time to stretch and get his head in the game. All in all, a very nice site in a very okay park, not rated wonderful because of the lack of full hook-ups (no sewer) and necessitating the visit of a honey wagon to dump him at least once in the two consecutive weeks he was allowed to stay. But satisfactory in every other way.

This morning Fish was cooking breakfast outside. It was still early but it was gonna be a warm one; July can still go either way in Central Oregon, but he was guessing 85 by noon minimum. He had the awning out, his rug down to keep out dirt, a couple of chairs out in case of visitors, his zero-gravity lounger on the other side of the sheet-metal fire-pit. The large dog pen, where Ray could hang when Fish was outside with him, was tucked back toward the rear of the site but still on the passenger side so Ray could see him and not mope too much.

Fish was cooking eggs and bacon and wondering what he had gotten himself into by agreeing to play in the two Oregon tournaments with the Aardvark. Being part of his local turf, he knew these two tourneys pretty well. The Pickleball Mania tournament, this one right here at Thousand Trails, was an institution, one of the oldest pickleball tournaments around, probably sixteen years continuous running by his count. It had come about through the efforts of some of the early pickleball pioneers, good solid tournament players like Bob and Beverly and Dee and Carl and Juanita, folks late in their pickleball careers now, but those still with us were still winning medals.

Fish poured a bit of the bacon grease back over the eggs to finish them and slid everything on a red plastic plate, along with a store-bought cheese Danish. Breakfast of Champions!

He balanced the plate as he leaned back in the lounger and thought about the history of this most unusual pickleball venue. While always physically charming, Pickleball Mania was a funky tournament in many ways. For years it was played on the worst possible temporary courts. They were concrete but broken entirely around the edges as if some sadistic creep had busted them up in the dead of night to make the outside footing, where you are really moving to track down a ball, the kiss of death or more likely the kiss of knee, shoulder, or hip surgery.

That is, they were that bad until recently, when Thousand Trails drank the Kool-Aid and made several of the virtually unused 40-miles-of-bad-road tennis courts into six of the most bitchin' pickleball courts Jon knew of. He had never seen the old ones, he started playing too short a time ago, but he thought part of what made them awesome-sauce was the fact that they were on a peninsula of grass bordering the Little Deschutes River, simultaneously occupied by families playing volleyball all over the place, dogs running amuck, owners certainly not doing anything to even read the numerous keep-dog-on-leash-or-you-die signs posted everywhere, and a population of ground squirrels equal to the revived population of the *Walking Dead*.

If they had thrown down a bluegrass festival right in the middle of this field it would have moved from maybe 9.2 to 9.8 or so on Fish's personal action meter, even though he wasn't really a bluegrass fan. He was very much a fan of synergy, and with all that action in one place, how could that be bad?

Over the last several years Pickleball Mania itself had also evolved a bit. It was now run by Dee as an honest-to-gosh pickleball tournament replete with only semi-funky online registration and the works. However, as often as not, Dee got into the act and started stipulating who was gonna play whom, and while you'd still see the top two seeds in a bracket playing each other in the very first match, somehow all that still worked, worked as well as did their serving gi-normous and gooey cinnamon buns for contestants on Sunday morning.

Because the tournament catered to players near and far, the locals were always having some kind of after-hours function, too, and players were going off to somebody or other's local house every evening for what seemed to

Fish, having only gone along once, as an excuse for consuming entirely too much booze for one small group. This calculation was based on the heavy contractor sacks of empty wine and beer bottles that came back into camp the next morning.

So what did this mean to his playing with Aardvark? Virtually nothing. There were, however, some advantages to this July tournament being the first for them. For one thing, they both owned RVs. This in turn meant that they would both stay there, and since practice play convened every morning at 8:30, and seemed to end around 1 p.m., within those 4-5 hours they'd both be able to explore if this was simply an exercise in futility, frustration, or stupidity on their parts.

In other words, they'd be able to feel all the stuff that anyone in pickleball feels agreeing to play with someone they haven't seen much, much less played with. And they'd stay together long enough to learn each other's games pretty well.

Which knowledge, Fish thought, they'd certainly need. He stopped for a second and got a pad of yellow paper and prepared to make a few notes. He wrote a title: 'Aardvark and me playing at PM.' He crossed out PM and wrote Pickleball Mania to prevent confusion. He thought about what he had seen about the Aardvark, and he thought more about how little he really knew about his own game, what he was capable of and all of that. He put these random thoughts down into a list for further use later:

~ *We are both left-handed. This could be made into an advantage. We need to think about that, how we can use it.*

~ *The Aardvark doesn't seem to have any obvious strengths. So I don't know how to defend him, or how we should attack against a right-left team or against a stacking team.*

~ *Dress codes? Try to dress as a team?*

Fish'd rather die ... that last line was crossed out in his

mind as he wrote it. He was not clothes oriented at all.

He couldn't think of a fourth thing.

He thought for a long time about this. He finally had to admit he didn't really have a bunch of even generic strengths, either for them as a team or for the Aard as an individual. You know, like 'great hands!' or something. You could say that kind of stuff until the cows ate the milkweed and still not know what it meant. Great hands meant nothing, near as he could tell.

The last thing he thought about had something to do with screaming. He was flashing on something now, something about them both doing a full-throat rebel yell at some point. Was that a rules infraction? How about after their winning a good point? Would that be considered poor sportsmanship, like a college or pro basketballer going to the glass and shattering it into smithereens? Besides, he wasn't sure what they had to yell about at the moment. Maybe it would come to him later.

Anyway, no doubt the tournament would be a learning experience. And it'd be fun. It was funky, a number of his friends would be there, and it would be unlikely that either of them would embarrass the other. That's what Fish thought right then, anyway.

Fish finished breakfast and put the plate on the ground in Ray's pen, where the good dog tongued it. *Have all the dishes washed by Ray. Put them back into the cupboard. See if anybody notices.* Fish loved practical jokes but he wasn't sure how practical that one would be, given that he'd be forced to eat off the plates as well, so as not to give the secret out.

The second tournament was a much different kettle of fish; weak pun, Fish thought, intended. The Pickleball Zone USAPA Pacific Northwest Regional Championships was a qualifier tournament. People who won there, or perhaps even came close, were winning a straight-up invitation to the Nationals. As of last year, the Regionals had also included a Pro Division, which, if he hadn't wanted to join their ranks, would have been meaningless to him and he assumed to most other people, but he agreed that the entertainment value of watching the best go head-on-head with each other was worth the small cost of admission.

He thought about how good those guys were, how hard he knew they trained. They were true professional athletes in a sport only beginning to be recognized for what it was, a difficult sport to play well. And they were each investing in the sport as well, as there wasn't anywhere near pro money as you'd compared to tennis. Or a bunch of other sports. Each one of those *other* players, in nearly any other sport, would be sponsored and they'd all be driving up to Bend in 45-foot Prevost motor homes, RVs with so much horsepower and torque they could pull up trees, all with marble-tiled floors, painted like abstract works of art, individual names in exotic decals on the sides.

He felt the old need in his stomach at the thought of Prevosts. People who owned Prevosts pissed him off. Or made him angry at himself for not having earned one. Who knows what his reaction was? Just 'clinging,' wanting something for no reason.

Fish was thinking Prevost for a reason. Wandering around the coffee shop at Casa Grande a few weeks back he had seen a brand new paper-plates Prevost pull into Casa Grande, gleaming like a friggin' neon-backlit rainbow, with something like a variant of Leanid Afrimov's color-dripping Rain's Rustle II hand-painted on the back, Fish having studied Afrimov's work a bit in college. *Fish,* he thought then, *you are looking at $2.5M on the hoof right there.*

Fish wasn't shy, no retiring forest creature. He walked up to the owner, a pot-bellied, medium-height Texan wearing boots and an eleven-gallon cowboy hat both colored, strangely, much like his rig, and after exchanging a few pleasantries and Fish's offering to teach the fat bastard how to play pickleball, he simply jumped in.

"I know it's rude of me to ask …" he began.

"Hell, son, it's not rude! If Ah didn't whant people to ahsk me, I wouldn't be drivin' the damn thing, now, would I?"

"Ohhh-kay, so …"

"$3.1M, son. Cash. You know much about art?"

Fish had, at least, minored in the subject. "A bit," he admitted.

"That's no photograph on the back. That's the real deal. Guy painted it right on there. Me and Sally, she's my l'il trophy over there, we like to call it Rainfall on Caprock Canyons."

Holy shit. It WAS an Afrimov! Painted on the back of an RV! He was looking at a motor home worth more than he would earn in his entire working career, including the lotto money his Nana had told him he would win. On her deathbed Nana had been quite specific about St. Joseph having told her that his wife, Mother Mary, had said Fish would win more than $1 million and less than $2 million, not including the tax bite. Who could disbelieve her deathbed revelation? He could almost take it to the bank, right? No, not right, but this guy was driving a rig worth maybe three times that amount anyway.

Envy grasped him in a way that almost made him gasp. He had tried hard not to hold onto things. When he did need to buy something, he was modest, even though he could afford better. Nonetheless, every once in a while the undeniably physical need to possess, own, achieve something got into his gut and went up his throat so that he could taste the bile. He needed that Prevost! He did! He would sell his home in Bend and put a good down payment on one! He could make the monthly payments from his pension. He could do it!

Instead, after a bit, he went home and drank two bottles of water, sat still, felt his breath for a half-hour and the feeling had passed. But even today when he thought about a Prevost there was a certain tingle deep in his belly, not entirely unlike the prelude to sexual excitement.

Did that have much to do with the tournament in Bend? He considered it. No. He wouldn't get rich, not the Fish. He was destined to live a middle-of-the-road existence, money-wise. But he still held onto that dream for the moment.

Back to his mental meanderings about the Bend tournament. There was a certain something the pros brought to this tournament. All the regular old 5.0s had to play with these guys, meaning there was, effectively, no 5.0 bracket, but there were maybe 120 of the best players in the U.S., intermixed without partiality across perhaps the most beautiful sixteen-court complex in America, and the sight alone would make a guy hard ... no, that's weird ... or at least envious.

So the Aardvark and he, Jon, would show up for this very prestigious, well-run, very good tournament, lots of the beautiful people around, a tournament where, in fact, he knew a lot of the folks, with him living there and all. So would their likely pathetic performance bring shame to him? If he played like he had played in the consolation rounds of this last tournament, and if Aard played as miserably as HE had played, then two-and-out would come quickly. But he would have done his best. Did he need to be nervous about playing in any tournament where he had done his best?

This was an interesting line of questioning. He took a few deep breaths. He breathed in two counts, out four counts. In two counts, out six counts. He checked his emotions.

He would feel no angst at all if he did his best, and he committed to himself, right then and there, that he would do nothing whatsoever about Aardvark other than be ridiculously supportive if he could find a way to do it. Clearly the fact that online he saw the Aard had been winning a bit didn't change the opinion he had developed watching him in Casa Grande. Nobody could play worse than him. Aard must have lucked out with great partners.

## Chapter Fifteen

LATER THAT AFTERNOON Fish and Ray took a hike down by the river. The route they took brought them along the edge of the Little Deschutes, giving the boxer ample time to choose between futilely chasing the ducks, looking ridiculous trying to snout out the big slow-cruising near-tame trout lazing in this no-fishing stretch, and occasionally paddling out to greet one of the parade of canoes and kayaks going through. Thank God this is a dog-friendly country, he thought, as Ray snuck up behind a six-foot mini-kayak and scared the bejesus out of a young paddler who wound up laughing hysterically when she realized what Ray was and yelled, "I thought he was a muskrat" at Fish. "I hate muskrats!" She paddled back to Ray and gave him a piece of a sandwich. *God, I love Bend,* he thought.

After more adventures than the young dog could count, Ray simply lay down on the grass, slumped his maw down between his front toes, and went to sleep. Fish was near dozing under a nearby tree when the glint of an incoming RV at the guard station across the river caught his eye. It was a small but spectacular Airstream motor home, maybe twenty feet long. Not a trailer. A motor home. Behind it the owner was pulling something on a trailer. It, too, was brilliant. Were his eyes both going bad? Was that an aluminum motorcycle behind an aluminum trailer? How cool was that? Flash on the tin man of *The Wizard of Oz.* The short, stocky driver got out to talk to the guard.

Delete the Tin Man.

"Hey, Aardvark," he yelled! Too far away. The Aard couldn't hear him, but no question it was him.

Jon tried pushing at Ray a little bit to wake him up. Ray grumbled a bit and turned away. Fish stared super-hard at his friend's choice of wheels. Most modern RVs are well-finished, but there is something about an Airstream that simply defies words. It isn't the same as the bewildering, mesmerizing opulence of a Prevost. A perfectly preserved Airstream motor home (which are quite rare compared to Airstream trailers, a fact Jon somehow knew) will still cost a buyer less than half the minimum down payment on a Prevost.

And what you get is surprising. Airstreams, motor homes and trailers alike, have aluminum bodies. There are certain beauties about working with aluminum. It's low density, therefore low weight, very strong (although within limits), malleable, making the curvy motorhome design not only possible but practical. It was corrosion resistant and easy to keep shiny, which the owners of Airstream RVs invariably did. The overall style is simple, graceful, and curvy and above all, gradual. Nothing happens fast over the design of an Airstream. No abrupt edges, no sudden starts and stops. Everything tapers into the next thing. You can see the riveted seams in many of them, but nonetheless they appear seamless as if it's all an optical illusion that they have seams at all, the infinity edges of the RV world.

Fish pushed Ray to his feet and began walking toward the rig. He wanted a closer look, he wanted to say "hey" to the Aard and exchange site numbers, maybe invite him over. But also, he wanted to get a close look at the A's toad, which now he could see more clearly really was a motorcycle on a trailer behind the relatively small motor home and could possibly be a for-real aluminum motorcycle. Fish was only aware of a few aluminum motorcycles. Growing up, he and his mild-mannered dad had worked on their two motorcycles endlessly. His dad had had a racing bike and parts of it were aluminum and shiny and other parts were cast and dark and together the look of it, Fish thought, had been killer. This was even better. He knew bikes and the only aluminum motorcycle he'd ever seen was made by Confederate, and like this one, looked space-age, all angles and edges and gears, like it was going two hundred miles per hour standing still.

As he got closer he saw that, yes, the motorcycle was aluminum, the RV was aluminum, and he couldn't swear to it, but it looked pretty darn likely that the storage box on the back of the RV was aluminum and if pressed he'd guess the trailer for the bike was all aluminum as well. All of which spoke volumes about something. Probably, once again, something about Aardvark. He walked closer to them and waved again. Aard was still talking to the uniformed gate person, them both leaning against the RV in the sun, enjoying its reflected warmth off the body of the Airstream. They were facing him across the small river but neither noticed, that engrossed in conversation. Fish leveraged up a large rock and heaved it two-handed into the river. Ray followed it in with an equal splat.

The two concussions got the men's attention; they both looked up, the ranger shielding his eyes, trying to get a better idea what was going on in the glare. Aardvark simply looked up, looked right at Ray, right over at Fish, and smiled widely. He put his hands together at about chin height, and bowed slightly, never taking his eyes from Fish. Fish did the same back, grinning a little inanely, he thought, but it's how the guy made him feel. Like grinning. How bad could any partner be, when he made you grin?

Fish walked across the bridge to the guard station, Ray trailing behind, shaking off river water and feinting at marmots. Fish walked up to the Aardvark, the guard having gone back to his station, and extended his hand. Aardvark winked and held out his arms. Hugging Aardvark was like hugging a medium-sized fire plug. His thick head caught Jon right in the chest. The strength of his arms was amazing, and Fish, no wimp, knew under no circumstances should he ever piss this guy off, or worse, see him in a dark alley. He had never, to his memory, been hugged by anyone as strong and solid as this guy with the huge guns.

"What's this?" he asked Aardvark, gesturing at his rig, taking in the RV, the trailer, the bike, all with a sweep of his hand.

"Where I live," said Aard, glancing over. "And all I own. My beggar's bowl."

"Your coach is gorgeous," Fish said, meaning it.

Aardvark nodded. "It is. It was given to me by an old business partner. I enjoy looking at it."

"Nice partner. What year is it?" Fish bent down, looking under the little rig. What a simple little coach. How artistically designed.

"Late 1977. Wait 'til you see the inside," Aardvark said. "Speaking of which, would you like tea? We haven't had time to talk, really."

Fish looked at Ray, who had walked over to the Aardvark and sat next to him, looking back at Fish. Ray was filthy.

"Love it," Fish said. "Give me an hour to clean up Ray and take a shower."

"Of course," Aardvark said. "I've got to hook up anyway. Bring a chair with you." He looked up at the sky, which was darkening, but no real clouds in sight. "Maybe we can still sit outside."

"I'll bring something," Fish agreed.

"Bring Ray," suggested the Aard.

Walking away, Fish had this thought. Being asked to bring a chair was ordinary in the RV world. In this alternate universe, you go to somebody's place for cocktails, snacks, dinner even, you bring a chair. But he had the strangest … maybe a thought, maybe a feeling, that he absolutely had to bring a chair if he'd want to sit down. He'd bet more than even money that Aardvark only owned one chair.

He shook his head, not to clear it, just in wonder. Nothing this guy did was ordinary. He, Fish, had gone on the road to have experiences, and even their meeting had been an experience, that's for damn sure. For the hundredth time he wondered, *what will it be like playing with him?*

## Chapter Sixteen

AN HOUR PASSED and the very clean pair headed for Aardvark's place, just a half-dozen sites east of them. He had quickly warmed up some frozen edamame, lightly salted the soy beans, grabbed his camp chair, and snagged the gifted bottle of Riesling chilling in the refrigerator. He didn't drink and when he had, he'd hated Riesling, but maybe Aardvark would like it.

Ray viewed the edamame as prey and continued jumping at the bowl right to the second they got to Aardvark's screen door. It was snapped open on its outdoor catch and the door behind it was opened wide; Ray trotted right up the stairs like he owned the place and strolled into the Airstream. Jon, ten yards behind, didn't bother calling him. Ray made moral judgments about situations and people in split seconds. When Jon walked in behind him, the dog was already up on A's Euro chair, curled up tight, seemingly fast asleep, keeping a half-eye on everything all at once.

Aardvark was seated on the rug in the middle of the Airstream's warm wood floor, a small brown-painted table in front of him. When Jon came in he passed a cushion up to him so he'd be comfortable on the floor. "I see you, Jon," he said.

Fish smiled back, put his bottle on the tiny kitchen counter and took the cushion, which his bony butt would soon need. "I see you, Aardvark," he replied, completing the ritual.

They sat for a moment in silence like two old friends. "You know," Aardvark said, "maybe it's a bit chilly to sit outside after all?" He pointed at the outside digital display which was now showing a nippy 50 degrees.

"Good by me," said Jon, who had forgotten his coat.

"Is what it is," agreed Aardvark, who seemed to like the phrase. "Green tea?"

"Unless you want something a little harder." Jon nodded toward the wine.

"Don't drink." Aardvark looked down at the warming tea, scooping the fumes toward his nose.

"Me neither, mostly," said Fish. "Which reminds me. I've been meaning to ask you if you've noticed something about us? The two of us?"

"C'mon, man. You're over-thinking the similarities, aren't you?" Aardvark looked up and grinned, reached behind him and scratched Ray under his jowl.

"Maybe," said Fish. Truthfully, that was exactly what he had been thinking, with them both being left-handed, wearing earrings, zinc ointment, Patagonia hat, and now with neither one of them drinking alcohol.

"You do know," said Aardvark, "most similarities are merely coincidence. This isn't 'The Murder in the Locked Room,' you know."

"I guess," said Fish. "but it's a lot of coincidences."

Aardvark shrugged. He placed a delicate near-translucent cup in front of Jon, a heavy ceramic coffee mug in front of himself and poured the fragrant beverage. "How come I get the good cup?" asked Jon between sips.

"You didn't," said Aardvark. "I try to only own one of anything. One cup, one mug, one (nodding at Ray on the

Euro chair) boxer bed. I like the mug better for tea. Keeps it warm longer."

They sat awhile longer. "How'd you guys do in Granite Bay?" asked Fish at last. The tournament results hadn't been posted, but he had seen that Aardvark had played with a 5.0.

"It was good," said Aardvark. "We made the medals, but that's not the part I enjoyed."

Fish cocked his head at Aardvark. "Really?" he asked.

"Yeah. You probably know Alan. He plays out of Granite Bay?" the thick guy asked.

Jon nodded. "Of him," he said. "I've seen his DVDs. And him playing, on YouTube."

Alan was world class, but of the older world class, a group of 5.0s with last names like Friedenberg and Kane and Hackenberg and Youngren and Hager who used to win every medal in sight. Alan was among them but after a point his hips had given out. Nonetheless, his instructional DVDs and clinics were in demand everywhere. And on a court on a given day, he could still keep up, maybe not as much as before, but pretty well, that's for damn sure.

"I played with him. He's fun," the Aardvark said. "Nice man. Smart, too." He took a moment to sip some tea. "We were down early in the first game. We took a time out and fine-tuned a couple of things. We won that game and every other game, as I remember."

"You got gold!" Fish exclaimed. His new partner had played in a 5.0 bracket and not lost a game!

"Guess so," said Aardvark. "Must have," he now amended, "now that I think about it."

"Show me," Fish ordered brusquely.

"Can't. Gave the medal to a homeless dude. In Auburn. I think maybe he thought it was money, or maybe gold. I remember he bit it."

"You're making that up!" Jon flashed a homeless guy, a sleeping bag rolled underneath his shopping cart full of black contractor's bags, his pit-bull cross on a clothesline trotting next to him, standard-issue homeless but with a gold pickleball medal around his turkey neck.

"Fish shoots, he scores!" Aardvark grinned. He reached behind him to his right and opened a small door in the built-in cabinetry. He pulled out a gold pickleball medal on a blue ribbon and handed it over. On the front it said 'Granite Bay Open' across the top and '2017 across the bottom. In the center was the head of a bear. Jon supposed it was the town's mascot or something. Jon turned it over. Engraved there was the proof: 'Men's Doubles 5.0.'

Holy schmoly. Jon felt fortunate to have gotten to 4.0. The medal certainly inspired more questions than it answered.

"How'd you hook up with Alan?" he asked, handing the medal back.

"You still don't know how to ask the questions you want answered, do you?" Aardvark poured a little more tea in their cups. He reached under the bench, took out a small votive candle, and placed it on the bench between them, lighting it with a kitchen match.

"You've said that," said Fish. "Not sure it's always relevant."

Aardvark thought, putting a finger to his nose like a dark Kris Kringle. "Yeah. Maybe nothing is always relevant."

The night outside was companionably dark. Besides the candle there was only one light lit inside the Airstream, a dim bulb in the back toward the sleeping area. Ray was snoring and snuffling behind them. It was very cozy in the little coach.

"Would you like to smoke?" said Aardvark, suddenly.

"Mostly I don't smoke," Fish answered, not completely sure what he was being asked.

"I enjoy being in Oregon." Aard reached again under the bench and pulling out a small box with no cover containing a row of perfectly-rolled joints. Aardvark took one out, rolled it appreciatively in his fingers, then leaned over and lit it from the votive candle. He inhaled deeply, held, exhaled even I've never seen anybody more slowly. "Legal dope is a good thing." His raspy voice seemed even deeper.

"You smoke dope like you're doing a yoga exercise," said Fish. "Did you know that was a perfect two-count in, two count held, four count out?" He took the offered joint from the smaller man's huge fingers and inhaled, trying the same count, almost succeeding.

"Yogic breathing. Huh. You are very observant," said Aardvark. He took the joint back, inhaled, held, exhaled.

"Some things, maybe," said Fish. "You are definitely not what I first thought." His turn again. In, hold, out. He felt a nice familiar buzz starting. There was a palpable shift in his vision, a lag when he looked around. He stared past the flame on the table at Ray, who had raised his head to sniff the smoke and then lay down again. He now noticed more colors in the coach, the aluminum inside, the cherry-warmth of the wood cabinetry, the red oriental rug under the edge of the bed toward the back. He looked at Aardvark, noticed for the second time now the — still reluctant to say it — aura around him.

Aardvark grinned at him. "Are we playing tomorrow morning?" he asked.

"Do you know you sometimes have an aura around you?"

This suddenly struck Fish as very silly and he started chuckling.

"We all do." Aardvark smiled sweetly. "You, too! But what about tomorrow morning?"

"Sure, we're playing tomorrow. 8:30 down at the courts. We can challenge in some, stay together as a team." He remembered something. "Do you want to try to stack?" he asked, referencing the formation where partners keep their strong hands both in the middle all the time, the middle being the normally most vulnerable area. In his and the Aardvark's case it was a matter of necessity. They were both lefties but Fish, from what he had seen, was so much stronger a player that it made sense to keep them in a regular place with him in the Deuce court. Plus, he could cover more for Aardvark from the right court if the heavy-set guy wasn't mobile enough to get to stuff.

Aardvark giggled. The sound was strange, distorted within the framework of such a rough voice. "If you want we can," he answered. "I think it might make more sense to play a little straight up first."

Fish had no idea what he meant and put it down to being semi-stoned. He got up, rubbed his aching quads, rinsed his mug, filled it with water from the kitchen sink, and looked around. He was struck by how perfect everything inside the coach seemed. There was no dirt, no out-of-place-ness. No visible unworn clothing, no dirty laundry, no garbage can even. He himself was a bit of a neat freak but only a bit. This coach would have made a brain surgeon's operating room look slovenly.

Fish sat back down in front of the bench. "Where did you meet Sam?" he asked.

When Fish had gotten up Ray had as well, expecting to leave. Seeing they weren't going to, the dog wandered over and sat next to Aardvark instead and leaned into him. Aardvark scratched behind his ears, his chest, then down at the base of his stubby tail. The guy knew something about dogs.

Whenever he stopped, Fish noticed, Ray would place his deceptively strong paw on Aardvark's arm and push down. When he did it the third time, Aardvark took the heavy gold medal off the bench and, adjusting the dog's ears, placed it around his neck. Ray looked down and snuffled the medal and then ignored it as if it were his right to wear it. Fish stifled a laugh, turned it into a cough.

"We met at Boston," Aardvark said. "At school."

"Huh!" said Fish. "Boston Medical? You a doctor?"

Aardvark snorted. "Well, some misguided folks have said I've healed them. But, no. Boston School of Theology. His son, David, and I were both on the minister track for a while. I met him at a parents' night one year. I don't have living parents, so I borrowed his. Hung around with them a little."

"David ... he's high-tech now, I thought?" Fish had a substantial flash of having met a man in Sam's office once, a man about the same age as he was, like a mini-Sam but taut, great forearm definition, full-sleeve tats on both arms, a few days growth of beard, altogether attractive and charming, lots of presence. He was sure that was David.

"He was," Aardvark said. "He retired. Same time as me, in fact. We started a company together."

"So obviously you didn't become a minister."

"Oh, please, shoot me," said the stocky man. "I did graduate with a degree in theology but I went back for some additional grad work. In computing sciences. Which David did, too, by the way."

Aard paused, looking out the screen door and across the way. Fish imagined he could also see the firepit burning at their neighbor's site.

Aardvark looked back from the door. "He and I were partners in a start-up, a little social media company. Nothing big, but we won the lottery and got acquired. We had had a deal when we started. If we got out okay, we'd buy each other something the other really, really wanted. I bought him an airplane. Beech B36 Bonanza. 2002, a few years old at the time, and perfect. He bought me this," waving his hand around at the Airstream. "Took him awhile to find it, he said. But it's what I wanted. Close to grasping material shit as I've let myself in the last few decades."

Aard climbed to his feet, went to the counter next to the fridge, and took the wax paper off a shallow dish. "Lemon bar?" he asked. He had cut the powdered-sugar diet destroyers into big irregular hunks, man-sized.

Fish would have climbed through broken glass to get at a lemon bar. "Just one." He took the biggest piece he saw.

# Chapter Seventeen

A BIT LATER Fish and Ray strolled back toward their RV, Ray peeing on various bushes and making half-hearted feints at fireflies and noises in the bush and Fish licking the powdered sugar remnant of several lemon bar hunks off his fingers. It was shaping up to be a beautiful Oregon summer evening.

It was about 9:30 p.m., he guessed, but not really dark yet. Around him he could hear the occasional fire crackle and a kid yell or screech, or was that that damn barn owl? He hoped for the former. At night there is nothing louder or more startling than a barn owl shouting right outside your open bedroom window. Even kids on Razors would be better than a barn owl.

They quickly settled in their rig. Fish thought about Aardvark. Friendly guy, nicest guy you could meet. Good dope, too, but Fish put that down to his just being in Oregon and having money to burn, pun intended. But now he knew some other stuff. Aard had made some money doing something tech-y, and obviously would share more information there if asked. Fish was good with that. Also, he and David were partners and friends. That validated the Aardvark, but it didn't explain him, did it?

That night Fish lay in bed, listening to the friggin' barn owl swooping occasionally by his window. As his consciousness subsided to a relaxed state, the rush of air from the owl's moving wings and the calm night brought a sense of something new about to enter Fish's life. The sensation, alive at the very edges of sleep, was almost that of a door opening.

Fish drifted off into a sound sleep and dreamed of alternative dimensions with red and grey doors and owls delivering messages to faceless people standing in front of and then walking through the doors. Even in the dream he recognized the Harry Potter books and the owl business, but it was a pretty swell dream anyway.

The next morning Fish worked Ray a good bit, got him settled in the Winnie, and was at the courts by 8:20. Aardvark walked on a few minutes after. The courts were vacant except for a foursome down at the end and nobody else was waiting to warm up.

Fish bowled slightly. "I see you, Aardvark," he said.

Aard grinned and nodded. "And I you, Fish!" he said. He undid his robe and tossed it on the arm-guards covering the ragged edge of the top of the fence. Under it he was wearing a t-shirt with his own image on it, or rather, his avatar, an aardvark, in this case one with the same shirt on. Fish walked over to him and bent to peer at the smaller image on the shirt-within-a-shirt. Yep, sure as Satan, another aardvark inside the smaller shirt, and so on. Like looking into mirrors facing each other.

"Cool shirt," said Fish after staring for a second.

"Want one?" said Aardvark. "I probably have your size in my pack."

"I'm good."

"You'll want one, you wait," Aardvark laughed, a prediction made with humor.

Fish smiled and rummaged around in his large backpack and pulled out a gallon-sized nylon mesh bag of balls.

"Do you know what ball we're playing with?" he asked.

The Aardvark smiled and shook his head. "No clue."

Fish walked down to the other foursome. Pit Bull was playing with a few lesser players and giving them fits, indicating he was in a good mood. "PB, what ball are we playing with?" Fish asked during a break.

"DuraFast 40. Got no idea why," Pit Bull said. That was in fact the ball they were already using on the hard concrete and in the early morning there were already two balls broken and laying out in the weed-filled lawn behind them.

Fish dragged a couple of the yellow tournament balls out of his bag and walked around the net. The standard warm-up in pickleball begins with dinking, an exercise in which each of at least two players stand opposite each other and hit soft shots over the net directly to their opponent. The ball should bounce in the kitchen, the seven-foot space between the net and the kitchen line where the opponent would be standing. Because rules prevent going into the kitchen and hitting the ball out of the air, each of the warm-up partners would allow the ball to bounce in their kitchen and softly return it. The philosophy is to start slow, allowing muscles to warm up and eye-hand to engage, before any deeper, faster shots are hit. Because the sport for so long had been the provenance of the Geezer-Jocks, Fish had always thought that that was about the best a Geezer could do, hit the ball slow, gradually engage mind.

But, truth be told, there is no harm in a few minutes of dinking practice. Dinking is an essential soft skill one needs to master. And, in fact, a drop shot from anywhere on the court even back on the far baseline, is nothing more than a glorified dink. Get your dinking down, you can play this game.

But what Fish thought when he dinked across to

Aardvark was nothing at all. A blank. He had so many competing expectations at this point that the Aard could have done darn near anything and he wouldn't have been surprised. Except for what he did do, of course. Jon, left-handed, dinked the ball to Aardvark's forward side, his left side, slightly to the side but in front of Jon. Aardvark picked up the ball off the bounce and dinked it exactly back to where Jon had hit it. Fish was pleased, returning the ball to a spot about six inches outside Aardvark's backhand side, the right side. Aardvark allowed the ball to come up, changed paddle hands and returned it to exactly the same spot on Jon's side.

This went on for a while. It's very unusual for an early morning warm-up dinking session to go more than about ten shots before somebody makes a mistake. *Hell, three shots*, thought Fish. That's the nature of things, after all. And why they call it a warm-up. But Jon was pretty good. Even with his bad eye and damaged peripheral vision he could keep up. Aardvark hit every shot back to the exact, probably mathematically exact, place where Fish had hit his. Finally, Fish couldn't stand it anymore. He lobbed a shot off the bounce, calculating the shot to go over the shorter man's backhand shoulder.

Except that it didn't. Aardvark made a lightning quick, graceful side-step back and to the side, set up and purposely hit the most outrageous shot, a lob off a lob. This shot is so hard to hit well that nobody does it, at least not regularly, not on purpose. You take the ball high above your shoulder and somehow calculate how hard to hit the ball to get it far enough back that your opponent (6' 5" Fish, in this case, with that 6' 8" wingspan to go with it) can't quite reach it. Otherwise you are sure to eat it. And then there's that pesky back line. And you only have fifteen feet to work with, between the kitchen line and the back line, to hit a ball that's twelve feet up and still keep it in. The math alone would tell you it almost can't be done.

Except that in this case the ball floated quite gently and seemed to stay up on some miraculous jet-stream for a very long time. It went just the tiniest bit above where Fish, side-stepping rapidly backwards, showing good form, could get at it in the air. But at last it dropped, like a rock, and hit the back baseline as squarely as if Aard had carried the ball back and dropped it from waist height. The ball hit the middle of the baseline and sat up in front of Fish, who was so surprised he didn't know what to do and so he ripped it into the net.

"How the hell did you do that?" Fish yelled at his partner, who was standing at the opposing kitchen line, watching the mini-drama play out and smiling sweetly.

"Do what?" the Aardvark asked mildly. That was a perfect answer whether he was trying to do that or not, of course. And what could Fish add to it?

"Good shot," he said. Aardvark nodded politely.

The warm-up continued. Jon moved from being surprised to bemused to nonplussed. He didn't know what to think, except that they might be in much better shape for a tournament than he had thought. For a 4.0 player, Aardvark had game. And in addition to having game, and here was the big game-changer for today, he had game with both hands. He didn't have a strong hand, as Fish's buddy, Noel the Mole, used to call it.

A-beast had *two* strong hands and was quick, quicker even than Fish. He could hit just about anything from just about anywhere, and certainly he could get to anything as well. He didn't always make every shot, but he got there and set up and tried to hit the right shots, and that by itself was more impressive than anything else he could have done. Besides, Fish reminded himself, Aard was only supposed to be a 4.0 ... really good but not great, not yet, but oh, so much better than he had expected him to be.

He felt his heart, held in check, loosen and lift. Not singing but humming.

It wasn't more than ten or fifteen minutes and Fish was beginning to get winded. He gave the 'time-out' sign across the net and walked off the court to his water bottle. Aardvark followed, getting his, a large half-gallon metal growler with a neoprene coating and what appeared to be the outline of an aardvark on it.

"You didn't play like this in Casa Grande," Fish said.

"Right Intention," said the Aard. "I remember I told you that then. Do you remember?"

"Right Intention doesn't have much to do with how you play pickleball."

"Au contraire, ma cher," said Aardvark. "It often has much to do with how I play pickleball. Probably should have something to do with your game, too, if you don't mind me saying it."

"So ... how you played in Palm Creek wasn't your standard game?"

"What? Standard? No." Aardvark laughed, dropping down to re-tie his still new-looking high-tops. "I was playing that way to remind myself of Right Intention, that this game is play. It's not a metaphor for life and death."

"Do I understand you?" Fish was genuinely confused but certainly intrigued. This was a new concept to him. "Does Right Intention here mean playing lousy pickleball?"

"Almost, grasshoppah. As I use the phrase, Right Intention boils down to accepting the many concurrent aspects of your life as it exists today. You examine how you choose to live and decide from there what is right to do in any situation. In this situation, I was playing singles. I don't play singles, I had never played singles before in my life.

"I couldn't have won, and lately I found I was taking myself way too seriously about this game. So I simply acted in a wholesome manner. My opponent was gracious and kind, so I would be happy when he won, and I simply went after every ball with an intention of swinging at it but without caring what happened to the ball if I actually hit it. In fact, wherever I could I closed my eyes just before I got to the ball and tried to see its path in my mind. That's something I'm not very good at, obviously."

"Holy … cow," said Fish.

"Well said," Aardvark replied. "Overall I knew I would hit some balls. And you noted today I can hit with either hand, something I wasn't born with but acquired as a different power some years ago. Now I'm literally ambidextrous, and have been for maybe — what — the last three decades? Story for another time, how I got there. But now I couldn't tell you which is my strong side. If I was guessing I'd say my right side might be 1 or 2 percent dominant, just a trifle stronger. So I was choosing to hit with my left side only. Which I can do, but my singles ground-strokes are very unpracticed left handed. Not to mention the closing-the-eyes part. Made it all that much more of a challenge."

"I had no idea!" exclaimed the Fish-man.

"Yep. I know. I didn't tell anybody. I didn't know anybody there, and I wasn't hurting anybody 'cuz I didn't have a partner. And I think it was great that my two opponents had a chance to win a match. I don't intend to be judgmental here, but I really didn't think either would have gone too far otherwise," Aardvark said, contemplating his paddle handle.

"You know," he continued. "Gotta say, that was the most fun I had in the whole tournament. To show up for the Duel and play left-handed with my eyes closed in a division I had never played in. My expectations were about zero and my enjoyment factor was considerable."

At this point Fish noticed Pit Bull and his own partner, Camino, tapping their paddles on the top of the fence. "You guys wanna play, or what?" said PB, not known for small talk. Well, except for when he answered his cell phone on the court. Fish remembered the first six months he'd known the guy, Fish had thought he was a doctor with a cell habit. Then he found out he was just thoughtless, but he loved the guy anyway. His wife Darcey was way cute, but beyond that ... PB was inexplicable.

"Sure, if you guys are ready to get beat," Fish said casually.

"You couldn't beat us if we gave you ten-to-eleven," the Pit Bull said.

"Beat you like a drum!" emphasized the near-monosyllabic Camino.

Fish glanced sideways at Aardvark, who looked as relaxed as an overcooked noodle. "Hope you don't mind a little trash talk." Fish turned with him to walk to the far side of the net. "These guys are sort of friends."

"I never trash talk," Aardvark said pleasantly. "But I don't care if anyone else does."

Trash talk is an interesting part of pickleball and Fish had thought about it often. In his mind he compared it to the supposedly more dignified game of tennis. In his experience there wasn't as much trash-talking in tennis. He thought part of that was because of the physical setup of the two games. A tennis court is 78 feet long and often all four opponents are that far away from each other in a doubles match. In pickleball, the court is 44 feet and one of the four players is almost always at the kitchen line by design, only 29 feet from their opponents if both opponents were all the way back. Thus, in pickleball you're dealing with a court that is constructed to have people almost twice as near, making it much easier to hurl a casual insult — in good humor, of course.

Any good pickleball player learned early to mutter insults just so they could be heard by the intended recipient without the audience or (in tournaments) worse — the referee hearing them, in which case the insulter could be warned of possible technical violations.

That said, trash-talk was often a part of the game, allowed in the same fashion as purposely trying to hit the other player with a body shot was allowed. Accepted and approved of, as long as nobody was really hurt emotionally or physically. This involved walking a very fine line and Fish had seen people hop over the net ready to throw down after some spirited repartee.

In fact, he once witnessed PB backed up against the fence by some pot-bellied ex-police officer pickler who thought it was a good idea for him to physically question one of the toughest guys in the game. That PB hadn't simply picked him up and tossed him over the low fence was a testimony to PB's wife, another reason Fish liked her so much. She could control his temper. Not many could, including Pit Bull himself.

PB and Camino got themselves comfy on their side of the net. Being on the north side, they served first, a convention on these courts. PB was usually first server, having a sound-breaking serve that carried weight. Second point in, serving to Aardvark in the left court, PB hit a good serve, a high arc, plenty of velocity, mid-court and well in, and plenty of top-spin. This was an intimidation serve which Aardvark handled nicely, casually floating in, short-hopping it, sending it equally casually back within six inches of the back line. Fish hadn't watched the Aard's stroke, but swore the ball had backspin. He had no idea how to short-hop and backspin the same ball. Anyway, game on, and so far, he was thrilled with his new partner.

The first game stayed near even, although PB and Camino had a huge built-in advantage, having played together many times. As partners they made very few mistakes although they each had tendencies that, after a bit, Aardvark seemed to realize could be capitalized on. Fish and Aard lost the first game 11-6, closer than the score made it sound, and Aard, without trash-talking a bit, simply said, "Nice game. However, I hope you don't mind if we beat you this time."

This is the kind of remark that some would take as facetious. However, it was as obvious to Fish, at least, that in this case he didn't mean it as facetious. On the change of sides between games, Aard tugged at Fish and they turned away from PB and Camino.

"Couple of things," said Aard. "PB wants to hit hard but he's been real close to the back line. Wind with us now."

Fish got that one. As he always hit hard, PB was more than likely to hit his share out, and with his temper, would often hit the second one harder. "Second thing?" he asked.

"Foot faults," Aard said.

"They're committing them?"

"No. We aren't either. But let's agree to call 'em on each other if we're too close to the line."

"Too close? We call foot faults on ourselves even if we don't commit them?"

"Yep. Within an inch or two, make the call. I'll explain later."

What the hell. It was only recreational play. Fish nodded.

Their serve and they got a quick gift as PB assumed Fish's big serve was going out and it didn't. As things progressed with the match, that should have been a tip-off for PB, but the Pit Bull didn't take the hint.

At this point, PB moved front to the kitchen and Fish changed sides to serve to Camino. Fish served to about mid-court, Camino hit it deep to Aardvark, who hit the ball about a foot over the net to PB. This sounds like a better return than it was, but to a powerful player like PB, who can get a strong hand on everything, it was a sitter. Fish gritted his teeth and purposely loosened his feet to try to get on whatever screamer PB hit. PB hit the ball full paddle and got the ball back, all right. Back to the back fence. On the fly. Point two.

It's too simple to imagine that from there on all they had to do was hit sitters to PB and let him hit them out. But PB might make that error and compound it by getting upset with himself and doing it again or doing something else equally erroneous. Fish knew that everybody does that to some extent, replay a bad play in their head right in the middle of the next point. Staying present is very hard in pickleball, a fast sport with little time for reflection, adaptation, or mental re-focus.

Still, both of their friends had to be thinking about these first two points and could, therefore, be slightly less aggressive. If so, Fish and Aardvark could feel free to ramp it up a little on their side.

But what really floated Jon's boat was that his partner had spotted the one thing those guys were doing wrong. In fact, another opportunity for a put-away came just a minute later. PB, trying to be conservative, short-hopped a dink and put a ball up a bit to Fish, who with his reach simply turned his foot a bit sideways and pounded it cross-court under PB and out, a clean point for the white hats.

Except it wasn't. "Foot fault." Aardvark's rough voice cut Fish's rosy glow.

PB and Camino glanced at each other. It was expected that good players call foot faults on their own team. But this one was unexpected as it was nowhere near an obvious foot fault. Still, it was Fish and Aard's call, and they had made it. "Thanks, guys," said PB. Camino nodded.

Although they had agreed to do this with each other, Fish was pissed. He had love, love, loved that shot! A player only gets a few chances a game to make a shot like this, and he only successfully puts them away in such a dominant way once a match or so. And his partner had just taken that glowing star of a shot away from him. He felt his stomach churn, the old familiar feeling. He breathed deeply into this. He gradually felt it going down. This was truly a Faustian bargain, agreeing to having his best shots taken away from him like this.

He reminded himself that he had agreed to do this. He didn't know why, but he had agreed to it. He nodded to Aardvark, placed his hands together briefly. "Thanks," he said. "Good call." Which was the right thing to say, in normal or tournament play.

The game progressed. They were very, very close; taking into account that one foot fault, which had obviously cost them one point and the opportunity to make another, they were neck and neck. Fish watched Aard more closely at the line. He didn't line up there as aggressively as Fish. He was maybe three or four, maybe six inches back from the line. Close enough, but with his arms being shorter, he gave up shots that Fish could have attempted to make. In any event, nothing came up that Fish could have called reasonably. Aard did find an opportunity to call another on Fish, but that one didn't cost them either as Fish had also hit the ball out.

Right at the end of this marathon match, however, another situation arose. They were on game point and in the play Fish noticed the Aard working PB, something not many people do. They were all at the line, which meant that he was returning every ball to PB, even balls that perhaps could be angled better to Camino. And PB, normally very aggressive on some of these shots, wasn't changing his pattern; he was simply dinking it back to Aard. And then Fish saw it, just before it happened. Aard was going around the post on this shot. PB put the ball up a little. Aardvark leaped sideways, to his left, across the lines to the outside of the court. That left him with a paddle on top of the ball and all he had to do was hit it without hitting or crossing the net. Which he did. And the game was over on this hero shot.

Except it wasn't. "Foot fault," called Fish. Fish wasn't sure, it was very close. But given what they had been discussing and trying to work on, he had to make the call anyway.

Aardvark glanced over and grinned. "Good call!" he said, nodding emphatically.

PB and Camino were dumbstruck with the call in recreational play. "Are you sure?" PB asked Fish.

"Pretty sure," said Fish.

PB and Camino both shrugged. What could they do? It was Aardvark's and Fish's call. Nothing for them to say, really.

Somehow, although the result had been even worse, them not immediately winning the game, Fish did not react as he had when Aardvark had taken that other point away from him. He was calmer about this. And to see his partner take the same sanguine approach settled him down even more. It was all good, right now.

The game took a while to end, but Fish now felt it was inevitable that they would win. And they did, some five or six minutes later, when they got back a point ahead and hit another semi-sitter to PB. Who, again, not having been overworked on hitting long but not having gotten over it either, hit it out. Game to Fish and Aardvark.

125

"Super play," Camino said at the net.

"You guys really worked it!" said PB, who always noticed good partner communication.

Aardvark didn't touch paddles this time. He put a hand on Camino's shoulder. "You are awesome, you are, really!" said Aardvark. "And," touching PB's shoulder in turn, "you ... wow ... what a fun game! We were so lucky to play you today!"

Fish realized that Aardvark meant all this. He really thought Camino was awesome, and Fish suddenly realized that, yes, Camino really was awesome. And, yes, what a fun game! And they won this game, too, although winning was hardly the most valuable lesson here, how to win. He didn't know what it was, but he was looking forward to a good, solid debrief with his partner.

The practice session and recreational play ended about 1:00 p.m., as Fish had forecast. He and Aardvark played together almost the entire time, certainly more than three hours. Not one time in that play did Fish feel as if he wanted to go try out somebody else. It was like finally finding your one-and-only after months of casual dating. Was that a realistic statement? He didn't know.

"Can you come over to our place tonight?" he asked Aardvark.

Aardvark rubbed his nose. "Sure. Maybe 7?"

"Six," said Jon. "We'll try the outside thing again. Don't worry about a chair."

## Chapter Eighteen

FISH SPENT THE AFTERNOON polishing his coach. Being in the presence of the Aardvark was intimidating enough in some ways, but his Airstream also gave Fish coach-envy and his Winnebago, just perfect for Fish's needs no more than a couple of days ago, suddenly looked tawdry and second rate. There was also the matter of Ray, and if they were having company as meticulous as it appeared the Aardvark was, they weren't gonna be sitting on a blanket of dog hair.

It's a mistake to think a short-haired dog like a boxer can't shed; it's another mistake to imagine that because it's not quite as noticeable it's not noticeable at all. Sort of like getting used to a particularly foul odor, imagining nobody else notices it either, and then discovering it was a raccoon having died on your exhaust manifold.

So, as these things do, one task ran into another. Thankfully he had bathed Ray the night before, one less thing to do. But washing the outside led to minor detailing, blacking the tires, polishing the rims, doing the windows, the front of the coach. Every insect south of Redmond was dead on the plastic film covering the paint and most of them had baked on.

Inside it was mostly the dog hair, but then it was also the tile floor, which Jon had a real thing about. Cleaning tile wasn't all that hard with only a couple of hundred square feet of it, but real tile, like he had, was much harder to clean than the more common vinyl, though there were tradeoffs. One of the positives was the lack of boxer scratches. Even Ray couldn't get through real tile.

But the negative compared to vinyl was the grout. Fish often wondered how the grout got so damn dirty. He took his shoes off every time he came in, his guests did, as well, and he at least wiped off Ray. As he was dumping his third bucket of filthy water down the shower drain he could only imagine what the floors would be like if he didn't keep them as clean as he did. But to clean grout properly required a small brush and lots of handwork and he didn't have that much time.

One thing an RVer can do at a campground is to use the campground's showers to save a little water. Not, he thought, like dropping in on his neighbor. Flash ... *May I use your shower? Thanks! I brought my own towel. Is this that new Head-and-Shoulders I saw on TV? Can I try a little of it?* Hilarious. He wasn't short of chutzpah, but a little bit short by that standard. Anyway, he got the coach and its interior spiffy-clean by 5 and he was in the park's communal shower by 5:15, wearing water shoes to protect against athlete's foot and thinking he should have worn a latex body suit instead; apparently, somebody had washed a pig in the shower just beforehand. But it felt very good to be clean again, and in clean clothes, only a little damp from his having placed his shower bag too close to the shower itself. Not so bad. He was almost dry by the time he got home.

He didn't know what Aardvark ate and this was a dinner-time invitation, although that hadn't been explicitly spelled out. This can be a problem among RVers. The general rule of thumb among full-timers is that visits last two to three hours, and if they occur between the hours of 3 p.m. and 6 p.m. there is wine, beer, and hors d'oeuvres, not dinner. This 6 p.m. invitation was on the outside edge of that, so perhaps more substantial fare would be required, and for some reason he felt uneasy and imposed upon. He took a breath. Held, released. Easy as ash falling off a joint, his anger disappeared. He wondered now if he was irritated because the guy would operate within his expectations and conventions? No, probably something would be different.

He did have an already roasted chicken, which was a good thing, and a lot of vegetables, a better thing. And brown rice. He put some water in a saucepan to boil. More in a teapot; he had some really great Matcha tea. He'd simply put it together and see what was up.

At a few minutes after six, Aardvark showed up holding a large white canvas bag. "I see you, Fish. And, ta-da!" He offered the bag. *If an aardvark could grin like a wolf,* thought Jon.

Fish returned the greeting and gestured to the floor, where he had arranged a similar set-up as Aardvark had set in his Airstream the day before. Aardvark folded into most of a full-lotus, amazing given his thickness, and placed his hands in his lap, bag by his side.

Fish placed the Matcha tea, already whisked, over ice with a bit of honey and put down their glasses at their sides. Aardvark picked his up. "I know this color. Is this Human Awakening?"

That was exactly what it was. "No." said Fish. "Guess again?" Aardvark took a sip. "Yes, it is," he said, wagging a thick finger. "Sage honey, too. Don't try to fool the Aardvark!"

Fish shook his head. There was a lot about this guy he didn't know; what he did know was that he liked him a lot.

The Aard took a moment or two before he commented again. "Did you ever talk with Sam?"

"Yes and no," said Jon. "I left him a ramble-gram and he

ultimately responded, said you were the real deal, whatever that means."

"Are you looking for a mentor, Fish?"

"I think so. But I'm pretty fixed in my ways."

"Did you enjoy our play today?" Aardvark asked?

"You know, I did. I don't know if it was just relief ..." said Jon.

Aardvark looked up at him and smiled. "Because we didn't completely suck, yeah?"

Fish thought. "True. But it was more than relief. You really seem to know the game. And you had us doing some interesting stuff."

"Like letting PB overhit with the wind? That was pretty obvious."

"No, more like the foot-fault drill."

"Why did I ask that we do that?" Aardvark asked softly.

"Okay, I see what you're doing," Fish replied. "But to answer, it made me realize that a single point, at any point in the game, means nothing. It kept me from being too serious."

"Would you be willing if I asked us to do that in a tournament match?"

"I put a lot of importance on tournament matches," Fish scowled.

Aard smiled. "No shit," he said. "I talked to Sam about that. Your serve and all."

Fish nodded, wondering why he was being so open with this guy he scarcely knew. "Yeah. So, could I follow your instruction and accept your foot-fault call in a tournament? I could try, I guess."

"How about if I called three foot-faults on you in one

game?" Aardvark reached for the teapot on the little hot plate. "You made three in one game today, you know!"

"No way! Are you serious? I didn't even make that one you called!"

"That's true, you didn't make the one I called. But the first game, bing, bang, boom. Three of 'em. Big feet, amped up!"

Aardvark got up, stretched in a sun-salutation, arms overhead, sat back down and reversed his legs, settled back in. "Not as flexible as I used to be," he noted. "Got a question. Do you do much journaling? Recording your experiences out here, that kinda stuff?"

"Off and on," said Fish. "I'm more likely to study tournament results, stuff like that."

Aardvark reached over and into the white canvas bag. "I've got something for you." He took out a largish book, weighed it in one hand, handed it over. Fish, with his accurate spatial eye, thought of it as maybe 10"x 8"x3", a slightly unusual size for an oversized book. It looked moderately old, had a fawn calf-skin cover, gilt edges. It was a beautiful book, uninscribed. He opened it. It had unlined, perhaps 300 thick pages. It was heavy, as if it contained more than the materials it was built with. And it shone. It had been polished to a gleam. Altogether it was one of the most beautiful books he had seen.

"It's wonderful, but what's it for?" Fish looked up at Aardvark who was watching him closely.

"It's for you," he said. "If you want it. For our journey together." He took another sip of tea, smacked slightly. "If you want that, I should have asked. The journey together part."

"And it's for journaling?"

"Yeah, or sketching, or whatever comes to mind. Way I

think about it, we RVers are nomadic sorts, and even if we play together some, that won't last forever. Sam said he had told you to be clear on what you are working on. We should get agreement around that, and as you see stuff happening that touches on those things, note them. To change anything internally takes lots of repetition, lots of work."

"Repetition?" asked Fish.

"Yep. When you see any indication of progress, especially." Aardvark paused for a second before he continued. "If you have a good serving day, what did you do that made it good? It's pretty unlikely it just happened. So write it down and be as specific as you can."

"I should write it down even if it's the same thing I wrote down before?" Fish felt more than a little confused.

"Well, yeah," said Aardvark. "Especially then. If you find evidence that the same thing worked more than one time, pay more attention, not less. A person needs to be alert for signs of new and positive patterns emerging. The new pattern might be a hint of a power trying to integrate itself into your psyche; you get me?"

"I see what you mean," said Fish, "but this is too much of a gift."

"Glad you like it, but I had a dozen. Part of the gift when I parted with David. Found 'em in the cargo compartment wrapped up like a Christmas present."

"A dozen?" Fish said. "These are very expensive."

"Well, it was a pretty good buy-out. Anyway, I've got eight left, after this one. I usually don't work with people as intensely as I suspect we might work together. I usually don't give these away. And I do honor that they were a gift. But you are … special."

"Sam told you … 'special needs,' right?"

"Right!" Aardvark grinned toothily in that Aardvark-wolfish way Fish already loved. "Let's make some dinner!"

Turns out Aardvark had brought a few things, a curry dish that smelled wonderful, a mango, some perfectly ripe avocados. "Thank God for Costco," he said as he took them out. "Thought I would show you something else, too!"

The thick man reached back in the bag and took out another book, a twin of the gift he'd given Jon but obviously not new. It was just as beautiful, but in the way scratched-up leather looks, not quite as glossy. Looking at it, Fish saw the book had that same strange damn aura around it, the same aura that his new book had.

"I call my books 'The Books of Common Wisdom'," said Aardvark. He opened it to the flyleaf and turned that page toward Fish. "See here? This is the fourth of my own." Fish turned the book and looked. Aardvark had written 'The Fourth Book of Common Wisdom' in a crimson color.

"Is that blood?" Fish said, shocked.

"Looks like it, doesn't it? But, no, it's just the color ink. I love that. Fools everybody!" Aardvark turned the book back toward himself and closed it carefully. "You don't have to name yours, of course. But I strongly suggest as your mentor that you write daily."

"I'll think about the naming part. I'm not in the habit of naming books, but did you notice …" Fish turned both books and looked at them in different lights, "they both …"

"Told you before," Aard said. "Don't make too much of the coincidences. It's probably the leather polish."

"I will write every day," said Fish to his new mentor, bowing to him, hands clasped as if in prayer.

133

"That's the spirit!" The Aard returned the clasped-hands gesture.

They wound up with too much food, which they ate anyway, with Ray offering to help.

"About the dog," said Fish at one point when Ray was right up in Aard's face smelling for scraps. "Feel free to kick him off."

"You are kidding, right? I had some pretty dark years when I liked dogs way better than people. And Ray's one of the good ones!"

"How about now?" asked Fish.

"Dogs versus people? 'Bout even, I'd guess."

"Well, okay. I don't want him to be a pest." Fish paused.

"No worries," said Aardvark. "In fact, let me show you something." He glanced at Ray, glanced down at his other side. Ray looked back at him for a moment and then dropped down, went around and sat on Aardvark's other side, the very model of a perfect gentleman.

"How?" started Fish. Boxers are definitely not like many other dogs, they do not have the Labs or Retrievers in-built desire to please; they tend to think things over before they agree to do them. And as well-trained as Ray was with Fish, he did NOT do with Fish what he had just done with a simple glance from the Aard.

"Just something he and I are working on. Rules of engagement, sort of. Sort of what you and I need to work on next."

Fish decided not to ask any further questions about the dog. But he did have something else to discuss. "Care to share anything about those dark days?"

"You think I was born this good-lookin'?" Aardvark grinned a bit. "It took a while for life to beat my rough edges smooth."

"So you had to do a little work on yourself?" asked Fish. "With a mentor and all that?"

"Yeah, of course. I was a mess. Maybe not as big a mess as you," he winked, "but pretty messy for sure."

"Who was your mentor? Can you tell me about the poor guy? Or woman?"

Aardvark appeared to think about it. "No, not right now," said Aardvark. "It's a bit delicate. And it'd be a distraction. For you, I mean."

Fish stared at him. *Delicate? Distraction? What's the big deal?*

## Chapter Nineteen

LATER, when Aardvark left for home, Ray insisted on following him, but in short order came straight back to his home couch. That evening, Fish sat with the dog's black jowls soaking his sweat pants, leaning his new book on Ray's head. He had never owned such a special book before. Everything about it was simple and gorgeous and built to last and the pages invited him to write every thought he had, although it had been a long day and he didn't have any really brilliant thoughts to write about.

"That's pretty much the way it will be," he decided. "Not everything in here is gonna be brilliant. But I can put down something every day."

He decided to write a little about the Aardvark's and his play together. Just a few words, but by the time he was finished and he took Ray out for one last pee, every light in the park was dark. He went inside and riffled back in the book. He had written five pages, plus a summary.

Aardvark had told him to look for positive patterns, things that he had done that had made a difference. He was surprised that he had written so much about one of those things that had happened prior to Aardvark's arrival on his scene. It was at Palm Creek, playing with Jeff, and that he had played significantly better after he had had his conversation with Aardvark. It was something about asking the right question. After he learned that sometimes he didn't ask the right question from Aardvark it became obvious that he should be more careful about his interactions with others. He had heard a therapist describe that carefulness as acting skillfully.

At the end, he went to the top of the flyleaf. There, in pen, a medium gel point, he wrote 'The Fish Finder' and underneath that, he printed in smaller letters: Volume One. He showed what he had done to Ray, who stuck his nose in his own crotch and groomed himself, boxer-speak for total lack of interest.

Fish had read many ideas about how many repetitions it takes to create a habit. For him, he believed that he should do something daily for about twenty days to begin to groove it and three times that for sure. So, for the first days, every evening, after play with Aardvark, after playing with Ray, after having a little dinner — sometimes eating with the Aard and sometimes on his own — he sat down, in the same position, Ray on his lap so he could use Ray's hard head to hold up the book and he'd note his thoughts, initially about pickleball, but soon becoming much more free-flowing and covering more than one subject.

Before long, he noticed that he was incorporating sketches into the material, to give him a frame of reference as to how deep he meant a shot would be when it was deep, or what angle worked on one player or another. He also included references about any other relationships and interchanges during the day, with the thought that his skillful acts there could also be replicated, making his life the richer for it going forward. Finally, he began journaling the tendencies of the other people in their interactions with him, and regarding pickleball, the interactions with his opponents. This was a lot of journaling but he was enjoying it. It didn't feel tedious or like an assignment. It felt good, as if he were doing it for himself, for his own self-improvement.

It was still a couple of days before the little pickleball

tournament there in Sunriver, but all the gang was in. In many respects Jon found the tournament environment invigorating and especially the week before, when everybody was playing everybody, no holds barred. This little tournament didn't have a lot of built-in elitism anyway; he and Aardvark pretty much stuck together, getting their own chops in, learning where the other was strong and not so strong.

On that subject Jon wound up incredulous every day. Aardvark had lots of game, lots of the time. He noted one evening in his journal that, *the guy has as much game as he wants to have.* He wondered what that would be like, that being way above where he himself was. Of course, Aardvark missed some shots, even sitters. Everybody does. But as newly-minted 4.0s they were expected to have a complete game, including all the drops, lobs, and even, as Jon had found, different serves. But if neither of them made every shot, neither did they miss a lot of shots, and when they did, as often as not, the other player was just a half-step in back of them, trying to get the ball back in play.

One note Fish made involved a play where Aardvark had allowed a ball to get outside his right side and he could practice hitting the ball around the net. The ball took him so far out, however, that there was really no chance of him recovering if he missed the shot. So, from six feet outside and back from the net, he hit a perfect drop shot back into his side of the net. Fish had been taken by surprise by that shot, figuring that he was gonna have to slither into Aardvark's court and he was way, way in, which meant that their left court was completely uncovered.

Except it wasn't, 'cuz Aardvark yelled, "Stay" and circled back around Fish deep and picked off the ball, which the opponent had hit deep to the ad court. They lost that point, but Fish didn't care. He loved the spontaneous thinking that Aardvark had displayed, the minimal but perfect communication with his "stay" call. It all made Fish happy. Happy to have Aard as a partner and happy to be able to count on him to do that right thing, having his back like that — in this case doing a right thing he didn't even know was right until he saw it done.

That night before dinner he took time to journal the day's play. The header for the day's entry read 'partner play.' As Fish wrote more and more, he realized just how important he was finding their increasingly regular communication. *Aardvark can cover anything,* he wrote. *But he does it in a way that that makes me feel important to the play. He doesn't make me feel like an afterthought or a hindrance. And I feel like I am empowered by that, somehow. I am willing, more than willing, to do the same for him. For us. Our team.*

He went back over what he had written and underlined the world 'empowered.' Not because the poor hackneyed word by itself was all that significant, but because the root of 'empower' is 'power' and it was a word he was looking for. Aardvark had set him in search of new powers. He didn't want to overlook the possibility that this empowerment was part of his search. He didn't know if it was or not, but he didn't want to risk missing it.

Later they convened around an open fire outside Aard's Airstream, the weather bit warmer. They picked at some baked chicken and plain salad, drinking tea, not even talking much.

Ray worked the top of the picnic bench, vacuuming every inch of it for food, hopping off once in a while to greet other dogs passing by. Fish often kept Ray on a leash when they were outside, but usually left the loose leash. For the most part Ray seemed to have an instinct as to when to greet a neighbor dog and when to leave it alone, and there seldom were problems. So for the most part the dog did his own thing around the campground, leaving them to talk or not talk, if they wanted.

It didn't seem like much of a night for talking from Fish's perspective, but Aardvark brought up a subject. "I noted that you liked our practice of Right Action," he said, explaining he meant the cover he had done across the left court.

"I did," said Fish. "But what do you call it?"

"A practice, an example, of Right Action. When you are wholly engaged in the game you know what to do. Your subconscious body understands where it wants to be and your conscious body allows it to go there. Right Action would be far more than that if we were exploring it from a sense of Buddhism, of course, but that's not what we are doing. We're thinking of it as coming up organically from a sense of play, of playfulness. Of doing what we can to make the play as fun as possible yet preferring it to be meaningful as well. The end result doesn't matter. It's only the action, or the attempted action, that's important."

"I sort of get that," said Fish. "Even though I think we even lost that point."

"I think we did," said Aardvark. "But the point was entirely unimportant, to me at least. It really meant that you were first willing to offer help when you thought I'd need it, and then that you'd be willing to accept help when you in turn needed it from me."

"There are probably lots of opportunities to help a partner like that if we look for them," Fish commented. "But isn't that just good partner play?"

"Depends," said Aardvark. "Sure, good partner play in any event, but when you give your partner room to do something out of the ordinary and look for opportunities to facilitate their attempt, you're doing more than just supporting them in their play. You're giving them a role model of how to act in other aspects of their life."

That night Jon wrote quite a bit, about the concept of Right Action as it applied to pickleball and also to life. Consulting his other books, he could see that from a Buddhist perspective Right Action was concerned with how people ought to act. Sometimes it was the search for a definition of right conduct (identified as the one causing the greatest good) and sometimes it was the good life (in the sense of a life worth living or a life that is satisfying or happy). In pickleball it was obvious now that Aardvark saw Right Action as something to be pursued on the court in first, how you act toward your partner (enabling him or her) and second, toward your opponent (encouraging their best game). But in either case he could see that it was intended to enhance the fun they had on the court.

## Chapter Twenty

THEY WERE A COUPLE OF DAYS AWAY from the start of Pickleball Mania and were on the courts early. Aardvark had said he had something to discuss. "I've been thinking about your serve," Aardvark said first thing.

"I've been trying not to. It's pretty good right now," Fish answered.

"And you know why it's good right now," the A answered. "It's likely to be different day after tomorrow."

Fish stared at him, no real answer available. "Suggestion?"

"Start serving backhand. Today," said Aardvark.

"I have an awful backhand serve," Fish said. "And we're two days away from the tournament."

"Consider it part of your Practice," said his mentor. "Capital 'P' Practice."

"So it's like an order?" Fish grouched.

"Only if you want to move past and arrive somewhere else."

"Have you been talking with Sam?" asked Fish suspiciously.

"Not lately," said Aard. "So, let's see your backhand."

Backhand serves are either natural to people or they are not. Fish had watched many people with excellent, even dramatic backhand serves and to him they seemed like

143

magic, so many moving parts, not simple-seeming at all. In theory, he knew, being left-handed, he would turn sideways to the right, allowing him to throw the ball up with his back (or right) hand, and hit it with his left hand, coming from low to high on the ball. The ball had to be struck below the navel and when the stroke was coming up, meaning no back-spinning the ball

He had overheard ferocious arguments on the court between people who believed that the ball could be back-spun legally and others claiming that to be fake news. Didn't matter. If you got the motion right, it was a serve that lined up exactly where you wanted the ball to go, and you had to go straight across your body so in theory you couldn't really get the yips and start hitting the ball over side fences and such. This made it a great serve for somebody with his issues.

But that was just theory. The problem was he had no authority in hitting it. People facing his backhand serve even moved into the court to take it early. He had seen them do it, but with his backhand serve he couldn't get the ball back far enough to make them wish they hadn't cheated forward.

All in all, it was a serve that had one benefit. If he learned it, he could get it in. And without talking about it, he knew what that meant to his Practice. It removed a point of fear from his life. Yes, he would rather have an assertive 'manly' serve, but everybody said it didn't matter, just get it in. And although he thought they lied, that in part it did matter, there was still something very real to that. You couldn't score points if you didn't get the ball in. The joke was that 100 percent of the shots one didn't get in did not result in points for their team.

This all went through his mind in seconds as he went back to the serving line. Predictably, his first practice backhand serves were awful, atrocious. Fortunately, the rest of the gang was late to the courts and they had time to practice. Aard patiently retrieved and hit balls back to him, making him hit the same backhand serve from the right court over and over, and then moving him to the left court and making him repeat the process, which over there involved a bit of re-alignment so was somewhat different.

He had never done such a concentrated series of backhand practice serves and was pleased to find that it did, in fact, become easier. That is, until they got in a game, and although it was still only a practice game and nearly two days away from the tournament his lack of comfort with the backhand triggered many of the same sensations as when he lost his normal forehand serve.

Uniquely enough, the shot would often enough go in anyway. The less comfortable he was, the less enthusiastic he was in his motion and the shorter the ball was. The problem with a short serve was that it brought opponents to the net and helped them run him and Aardvark all over the known free world. But if he could get it even moderately deep, then there was so little forehand spin for the opponent to work with that the ball never came back in an overly aggressive way, and if the opponent tried a hard return, as like as not they'd overhit it, often out of bounds.

By the end of the practice session he was getting almost every backhand serve in, not necessarily deep, but in, and he was getting increasingly comfortable with it, a little deeper each series. "I've got it, mostly," he said at one point six games down the line. "Can I mix it with my forehand now? So I don't forget how to hit a forehand?"

"Nope," said Aardvark.

"Well, when can I, then?"

"After the tournament," his friend said.

Jon looked at him. "That's crazy," he said. "I don't want

to serve backhand in the tournament."

"Practice with a capital 'P'," said Aardvark.

"You play that mentor card one more time …"

## Chapter Twenty-One

THE MORNING BROKE BRILLIANTLY over the Little Deschutes River. Fish and Aardvark were on the courts by 7 a.m., still working mostly on Jon's serve but mostly just getting a thorough warm-up. Some of the other players arrived soon thereafter, and well before the 8:30 start the courts were full of people waiting everywhere for an open spot. One thing they both knew about tournaments was there's lots of standing around, lots of waiting between matches, too little time to warm up, every real possibility of getting out there cold as ice and having the match be gone before you knew you were playing.

They were playing in the tough 4.0 bracket. Their first match was against two folks they had played several times during the preceding week. It was interesting how much more seriously they all took the tournament environment, but it made no real difference. Fish and Aardvark were a much stronger team and won in two games relatively easily. Fish couldn't believe how prepared he felt. He had never trained even *this* hard for any pickleball match and training with one partner was awesome.

There was only one negative in this match, and it was, of course, Jon's serve. Backhand, he easily missed a third of his serves. Did not get them in, typically hitting them short. The good news was that his feelings of spontaneous combustion from frustration or from events beyond his control were not there. The serves were short, that's all. And he would have had them in if they had gone just another foot or so. All the balls unfailingly were in line with the center of the target court, meaning he was aiming correctly and not 'yipping' or pulling up on the serve. He was, however, overly tense and each time he missed a serve he got a little more tense.

At the same time, he was gradually making better serves through the mechanics of practice so his mental state finally evened out. Giving away about one-third of his potential points as server was huge and would normally be a game-killer except here, with this partner and using his methods, it was not.

They never discussed Fish's serve during the match. It was Aardvark who did not want to talk about it, suggesting they wait until after the tournament. But this time while they waited for their next match, Jon did want to talk about it.

"I'm still hitting those serves short," Jon accused.

"This isn't my fault," said Aardvark matter-of-factly. "And since I, in fact, don't care that you are missing serves, why should we talk about it at all?"

"Maybe we can figure out what else we should do."

"Or maybe not," Aardvark said. "So why worry about it? We're winning without needing any more from your serves than we're getting, aren't we?"

"One match. But there's a lesson here, isn't there?"

"Of course. But you aren't ready to hear it yet."

"Give me a hint." Jon expected to be dismissed but instead he got something. "Pay attention to the rest of your game," Aardvark said. "See what changes in your game, if anything."

Jon thought about that. So far he hadn't noticed anything, but possibly he hadn't been paying attention. He relaxed a bit. Then, out of habit, he started concentrating on his breath. Soon he was someplace else entirely, someplace with bagpipes. *It takes somebody pretty good to play "Amazing Grace" on bagpipes,* he thought. He came up through the meditation to see Aardvark's face about four inches from his own. "We're up," said Aardvark. "We're playing Big and Little. Court Two."

Jon nodded, drug his journal out of his bag, and looked at the ideas they had formed the evening before for playing Big and Little Wolf. The Wolf brothers had been playing together a long time. Big Wolf was in fact the smaller of the two and Little Wolf was huge, more like a Cape Buffalo than a wolf. They played a nice controlled game. Their weakness was their lack of mobility. Big Wolf had good hands but couldn't move well laterally due to an obviously painful recent hip injury, and Little Wolf was enormously strong but simply couldn't move backwards quickly. Normally Little's lack of quick wasn't an issue as opponents had to lob sky-high to get the ball over him.

But Jon and Aard had practiced that. Their game plan was to bring the two Wolfs to the line and then lob Little. They assumed Little could shuffle back enough to get a paddle on it but couldn't hit it hard so he'd simply hit it in, at which point whichever one of them received the shot would hit it cross-court away from Big Wolf and the point would be over.

That was the theory. Jon didn't know much yet about making up game plans, but he did know that whatever you planned wouldn't happen. Yet it seemed that it would be generally better to go in trying to do something than just burn off five or six points looking for some weak point. And in point of fact they were never able to accomplish the exact scenario they had planned, not even once. Not that they didn't try. Big was moving better than they thought he had in the first match and Little was getting enough paddle on the lobs to make their jobs at the net pretty hard. The game was roughly even, but the Wolfs won it when Aardvark surprised everybody by calling Jon on a foot fault on game point.

"I wasn't even all that close to the line," Jon hissed between games.

"True, that," said Aardvark. "I just wanted to do it."

This was the weirdest thing Jon could remember happening to him on the court so far, save for his reaction, which was just annoyance, not seething anger. "Do you mind if we go beat these guys now?" he asked.

"That would be easy," said Aardvark. "Remember our plan?"

"Sure, but it isn't working."

"Sure it is. We tried the same play so many times that Little is hanging back, and Big is set to move left or right. So let's just lob over Big every time. Watch what will happen."

It was like a miracle. The first time they got the brothers to the line Aardvark hit a perfect lob over the smaller brother's backhand. Big was absolutely flat-footed and simply watched the ball to see if it was in. "Nice shot," he said, looking at his brother nervously.

This shot worked amazingly well twice more, and then Big began to expect it and started shuffling back before the lob was even hit. At which point Aardvark simply dumped the ball over the net and Big was caught flat-footed again, this time moving backwards. They did that a couple more times, dumping a dink when they caught Big on a back foot moving backwards, and each time the smaller Wolf couldn't recover fast enough to cover the ball. The score was 6-0 for Jon and Aardvark before the other guys knew what was happening.

From then on it was more of an opportunistic free for all with each team watching what the others were doing and trying to capitalize when they saw something. Toward the end of the third game, the score was in favor of Fish and Aard but not beyond reach of the experienced Wolfs. At that point Aardvark began faking backwards steps and sideways lunges the instant before the opponents hit a return.

Interestingly, both Wolfs initially went for these fakes and Fish and Aard got a couple of quick points. And there they were at match point with Fish serving. Aard called time out. Fish went to the back fence, facing away from their opponents. Aardvark joined him.

"Are you ready to win this match?" asked the A.

"Yep," said Fish. "Let's do 'er."

"Or not," Aardvark said. "Isn't this is a little too easy?"

"It hasn't been that easy. We're in the third game."

"These guys have not given us their best game," said Aardvark. "We haven't learned what they have to teach us!"

"I really don't want to throw the game, you know."

"I know. But what would happen if we … say … extended the rallies?"

"What?"

"We don't put anything away. We wait for them beat themselves on unforced errors."

"Are you seriously recommending this?" asked Fish, somewhat shocked.

"I have a hunch it'll be fun."

Fish looked at his partner. "You're crazy, but you're the

boss."

Aardvark smiled. "You can be such a good sport sometimes."

Extending a point can be a real strategy anyway, as they both knew. It can change the momentum. In this case, the first two points after time out were slightly longer rallies and both Big and Little made simple unforced errors, one into the net, one just a bit out.

After that, though, it was as if Big and Little got the memo. They started showing what made them a good team. And what ensued was some of the best pickleball points Fish had participated in. Previously they had had Big and Little Wolf off balance but now each rally was an event, fifteen, even twenty shots for a point. Soft game for a while, usually a lob to back off the other team, maybe a couple of body rips. Suddenly everybody was getting everything.

As this went on, Fish got more and more into a rhythm. He could see where each ball was going to be hit and was moving there even before the stroke was finished. He knew with absolute confidence that he could get anything hit to him and so he began looking outward at how he could better back up Aardvark as well. He began making outrageous shots as if they were his due.

Fish had always thought that one of the hardest shots in pickleball was to move forward aggressively from mid court to get a ball dumped just over the net, to stop before you get there, calm your body and softly dump the ball back. In this situation Fish found himself rushing forward with a completely extended paddle, with no time to stop and no lift left in his body. He'd wind up having to use wrist to lift the ball, always dangerous. For him, using wrist could be so hard to calibrate. He'd flip the ball up, right into the opponent's wheel-house, and eat it.

Not this time. Fish was literally mid-deuce-court and almost in back of Aardvark, having gone there to add an assist on a shot he knew Little Wolf was going to rip through the middle. Aardvark had also seen the shot was coming and amazingly had gotten it back soft and center, into that magic 'horseshoe' area where most returns are safe, but that caught Fish with his momentum moving right-to-left, leaving the right court uncovered. Later Aardvark would tell him that Fish had given him a 'stay' hand command and he therefore hadn't tried to cover it, but Fish never remembered any of that. What he did remember was Big Wolf, who took Aard's return and dropped it very softly just over the net at the sideline Fish had just vacated.

Fish had started for that corner even before Aard had shown where he was hitting the ball. He never looked anywhere else at all but at that corner, but at the same time he knew with a certainty that Big would step in from his own left court and roll the ball oh-so-softly across to his opponent's right corner. Aard was at least 15 feet away from that shot when Wolf went to hit his return. The crowd, totally into this terrific point, went silent when they saw the opportunity Big had. Big made the shot. Everyone knew this point was over.

Fish did not try to get all the way to the ball. When he got as close as he could, he instead planted his left foot pointed forward and stretched the tip of his right foot. He shifted the paddle to his right hand. He managed to get the paddle to the ball but had nothing left to hit with and was going to flick with his wrist, but for some reason, at that last moment, he slid his planted left foot toward his right, kept a very stiff arm, straightened his bent right knee and used the up-action of his straightening knee and stiff arm to lift the ball back to his right corner.

That he hit this shot at all was amazing. That he hit it with his off-hand said more. But the ball itself, clearing the top of the net by a fraction, had no momentum on it and simply dropped straight down, bouncing fractionally in Big's court and laying still.

This shot was too cool for school and for almost twenty seconds nobody in the crowd recognized what they had seen. When they did, it was pandemonium, craziness. Fish looked at the ball and didn't know what had happened. He did know he really didn't want the point to be over.

More, Fish hadn't realized that this was match point. He had hit this shot at 19-18. They had won the match on the best shot he had ever hit. They had won the match on what was, judged by the roar of the spectators, a great shot.

Fish had to ask the same question twice. "That's it? End of match?"

"Yep. And you were completely in the zone, grasshoppah," said Aard. "Pretty fun, isn't it?"

What Big and Little realized was that they, too, had played their best and that that last point could have gone to either team. Somehow, Fish knew, they were feeling pretty good about the match, although it dumped them into the Consolation bracket.

"You guys will be back," Fish said. He meant it and hoped it.

Big and Little touched paddles and waved to the crowd. They would be back.

Aard and Fish gathered their water and gear and went off the court. Fish didn't know what to say. He knew that in that last match he had played correctly. He had played the way he wanted to play, and that deep down he knew he had played as best he could play right now.

"Why can't I play that way all the time?" he asked out loud.

Aardvark didn't say anything, just grinned a little.

Is it possible that, after only two matches, the rest of the tournament could be anti-climactic? In a way it was true. The inner knowledge Fish had just gained of his own capability stayed with him, although the sheer certainty that being in the zone gives an athlete gradually dissipated like a chemical high fading from his body. He had the memory of it, but he knew he wasn't there. The thing that bolstered him was the possibility that he could and would, somehow and someday, get there again.

## Chapter Twenty-Two

THREE MATCHES LATER, Fish and Aardvark won their first 4.0 tournament.

They saw Big and Little again in the finals but this one was a nothing-burger. Neither opponent had shown up for the first game with Big's hip obviously hurting. This got worse to the point they had to withdraw mid-way through the second game. Probably this day it would have made no difference. Everybody knew Fish and Aard were winning that medal. It was their day, no doubt.

And in a way, this was arrival. 4.0 is the starting bracket for the really good players and winning any 4.0 tournament is special. But arrival is one thing and feeling that you had arrived is something else again. Aardvark and Fish found themselves alone, as usual, with Ray that evening, outside Fish's coach this time, with a bonfire between them and a lot to talk about, along with a willingness to not talk at all, as if words alone were unnecessary.

"You do get one," said Fish after a long while.

Aardvark, who was lighting a celebratory joint, didn't look up. "One what?" he asked eventually, examining the lit tip as he would a great cigar.

"One 'I told you so,'" said Fish.

"Told you so," said Aardvark. "And feel free to lay that across the several places I could have said it," he added.

"It's been decades since I was in the zone like that," Fish said. "Once or twice in high school tennis. I didn't even see it coming. I just kept playing better and better. Lost track of time completely. Didn't even know where we were in the match."

"Yep," said Aardvark. "That pretty much describes it."

"Can our Practice cause that to happen more often?" Fish asked, drawing the capital 'P' in the air to make it clear what he was talking about.

"Nope," said Aardvark. "I think about the best you can hope to do about the zone is to have fun when it arrives. Mostly I think we all win with our 'B' games." He passed the joint over to Fish. "I do think the Practice makes our 'B' games better, though," he added.

He took the joint from Aardvark, drew deeply, and watched the crackling fire. He didn't feel any sense of elation over winning today. He didn't feel victorious. It was more like a tough job well done.

Behind them Ray was having some kind of a boxer dream, lying on his back on his pad, kicking his feet in the air and howling in a half-hearted dreaming doggish kind of way. Fish had read that dogs dream about the same kinds of things that people do. He wondered, watching the dog, how the scientists could study that. He smiled at how little he knew about anything, really. And how little that mattered in his life.

Fish and Ray went out for a run the morning after the tournament. It was a nice day and early enough that Fish could assume there'd be few off-lead dogs, so Fish slipped Ray's lead off and let him run. They followed the Little Deschutes River trail down from the camp to the point where the smaller stream intersected with the Deschutes River. A light fog made everything near the river a bit hazy, which in turn inspired Ray to go into the fog as many times as possible in case he had missed a rabbit or better, a covey of quail.

Fish let Ray handle his own business and thought about what things he had written in his journal late the evening before. He had written a lot about how he learned. He was finding that in most situations he already knew what he should do to improve himself and come closer to Right Action. For him, the best approach to change was constant repetition. He didn't know if winning 4.0 gold would qualify but he did know two things for sure. One, he had missed fewer serves than his normal 30 per cent in the games they had played with him serving everything backhand. This was of course the biggie and knowing he could do it seemed to lift a weight off him. Even if he went back to serving forehand, he knew he could always get a backhand in if needed. He could serve and he didn't have to be thinking about it.

The second thought was simple; playing with Aardvark helped him play clearly. Aardvark had a magical way about him; he was non-judgmental yet still very competitive. If Fish needed something, Aardvark usually had it — a strategy, a focus word, a slight change in the pace of the game, a time-out, something Fish usually didn't call as quickly as was needed. Aardvark helped him achieve Right Action by encouraging correct repetition through practice and modeling better behavior.

This last thought made Fish wonder how he would play with other partners, given the things he had learned were in part related to how he played with the Aard. Fish wasn't given to compulsive thinking, but he found he had been visiting this issue over and over again. Not that he had any answers to it. Not that the issue meant much anyway. He knew he would play with people other than Aardvark and not that far in the future, either. He would see what he carried forward when the time came.

Coming back up the trail toward the camp, Fish saw Aardvark was in his little motorhome, slowly bouncing down the road toward him, towing his motorcycle on its trailer. He rolled down his window. "Gotta take a little trip for a few days," he said. "There's a guy who needs me to help him through a rough patch."

"Wow, really?" said Fish. "I have a bunch of stuff to talk about with you!" He leaned on one side of the driver's window and let Ray stand up on the other.

"Yeah, well, hold those thoughts," he said. "Or better yet, write 'em down. I'll see you up in Bend in a few days. We'll talk then." He scratched Ray behind his ears. "If you want, I'll take the dog off your hands 'til I get back." He smiled lopsidedly.

"We're good," Fish smiled back. "We'll look forward to seeing you!" As he said it, he realized that he meant it. He walked back toward his camp with Ray. For the first time in a long time he felt … he didn't know … lonely. But it felt good, too. Lonely and good.

That evening he and Ray sat by themselves near the campfire. It was very dark and quiet. Jon wasn't thinking about much, just watching the flames. In them he could see himself and Aardvark but he wasn't sure what they were doing. He smiled to himself. Nice to have a friend, he thought, his loneliness, for a moment, gone.

## Chapter Twenty-Three

THE NEXT MORNING Jon packed up and headed north through Bend to the Bend-Sisters RV Park out on Highway 20 and got Ray and himself squared away. This was their shake-down park and the young dog set about refamiliarizing himself with the area, including visiting the nice fishing lake. Fish wondered what a dog thought about trout. Did Ray see them as prey?

Jon called his parents to set up a dinner for the following evening and then Sarah to book an appointment with Sam. "Haven't heard from you in a while," Sarah said.

There was something in her voice. "Things okay?" Fish asked.

"Sort of. Or not. Not sure." She paused. "Don't be surprised when you see Sam," she said at last.

Wow, a big flash, a little rare for Jon these days. He saw a glimpse of a much older man, stick-thin, walking somehow strangely, wearing a round hat like a bowl. He didn't think any interpretation of that could be good; Sam sick? Maimed? He didn't ask questions. He put the appointment Sarah gave him on his phone's calendar.

The following day he arrived early at Sam's with donuts. Sarah saw the Sparrow Bakery logo on the bag and smiled big. Sam thought she was looking thin and said so. "You made my day," she said. "And he's not here yet. He said to go in."

Another card was taped to his chair. Like the first one, this one had a character drawn on it. A stick-figure of a person. There was a torso that looked to have clothes and a hard-hat like a construction worker's, but otherwise the figure seemed unclothed. The figure was stepping forward, the legs doing the stepping, while the body seemed to lag behind like the 'Keep on Trucking' man. He took the card and turned it over. Like the previous, the same inscription: 'Keep This Card!'

Jon smiled and stuck the card in his shirt pocket, turned to put his feet up on the other chair, and closed his eyes. *Same old*, he thought, following his breath while he had a moment.

Later he'd realize he had dropped into a profound meditative space. For a moment and for the second time he heard bagpipes. He opened his eyes into a strange space, a wide valley between two low hills. It was quite green. A crowd was in the distance. Again he saw the thin, older man from his recent flash walking toward him. He was carrying something. A bag of some sort, Fish thought. By the way he held it, it seemed heavy. It swung with deliberation as the man walked.

He woke from the dream feeling disoriented and detached. Sam still hadn't arrived. He felt a strange anxiousness, almost a panic. Reflexively he touched his shirt pocket. The card was there. He took it out and turned it around in his hands. The stick figure on the card was the same one as in his flash and in his dream. Too coincidental to mean nothing, he thought.

He heard Sam arrive, ask Sarah for messages. The man came in with a jelly donut in hand. "Thanks for this," he said. "Just what I needed," patting his stomach. "And what can I do for you?"

"Checking in," said Fish. "What is this?" He waved the card.

"How did you and your partner do in Sunriver?" Sam ignored the question.

"We won. But I think you already knew that, huh?"

"Of course. But tell me about it anyway."

"Learned something, I think." Jon smiled. "Maybe a couple of things."

Sam smiled back at him and leaned forward. "Seems your plan might be working," he said.

"Might be," Fish said. "Must be some reason I'm here, though."

"Your next step," Sam said. "May I see the card I left you?" He turned the offered card over in his hands, staring at the drawing. "Remarkable."

"How could that be?" asked Fish. "You are the 'artist,' right?"

"Si, Pepe!" Sam nodded. "Which doesn't mean I always get things correct. But I see things, too, from time to time. In fact, I had a dream last night that reminded me of this. I woke up thinking of you."

"Huh. Does it mean more for you?" Fish asked.

"More than what?" Sam asked. "Clearly we both had someone thinner than average in mind. Beyond that, the coincidence of both you and I sharing a vision, if you will, is too remote to be computed."

Fish nodded. He agreed, it was too strange to imagine that he and his shrink would see the same thing.

Sam rooted around on his desk and found a blue-lined paper tablet covered with writing. "You know, when Sarah said you were coming in, I went over my notes from our last session. Can we talk about that?"

"What's there to talk about?" asked Fish, genuinely curious.

"I made a short list after the session of where you were at that time. You might remember the items that were most critical to you?"

"Not sure I remember everything."

"Yeah, well, you were in a lot of hurt. Says here ..." he looked down ... "you were thinking your life was a mess." He smiled. "Hated your life, your house, your job, your parents, no relationships to speak of, no wife, no girlfriend, retiring, and not looking forward to much of anything."

He paused and looked at Jon, who was crossing and uncrossing his legs and arms. "You seem like you feel much better now!"

"Actually, I do," Fish agreed. "Some, anyway."

"What's still to be done?" asked Sam. "What are you working on?"

"You sound like Aardvark. Or him you," Jon said. "I think being retired and into the whole pickleball family thing works for me, so that's better. And I think Aardvark and I are becoming friends and I don't think I've had a close friend for a while."

"A while?" asked Sam.

"Okay, okay. A long while. And it seems I've worked through the serve thing and I can play pickleball now. Pretty well, anyway."

Sam nodded, looked back at the pad. "Girlfriend? Parents? Your eyesight?"

"I don't think about my parents as much. I mean, I certainly am not worried about them. And they don't seem worried about me, which is a plus."

"You didn't mention girlfriend," the therapist said.

"Nothing to mention," Fish shrugged. His few days with

the woman in Casa Grande flitted in and out of memory. *Wonder what she's doing?* "I'm thinking more about it, though."

"Well, that's a start." Sam thought for a moment. "Have you given any thought to faith?"

"Whoa," said Fish. "You mean like God?"

"Yeah, like Him. Seems to me He's a part of this."

"I haven't given it any thought," Fish said pensively. "I recognize it isn't really resolved for me, but I've got time."

"You only have," said Sam mildly, "all the time you have. In the meantime, I think being on the road is doing you some good. And I think the Aardvark is doing his part. But I wouldn't mind you having some different guidance."

"Guidance? Have you set up another life coach for me?"

"Nothing so heavy-handed," said Sam. "But this ..." he shook the card ... "will show up in your life before too long, I'd guess."

"So, you think I really need to do more ..."

Sam thought for a moment. "I don't mean to minimize what you've done already. You were leading a very painful life. Now it doesn't seem so painful."

"But?" injected Fish.

"But you said wanted to move toward something. Maybe more fulfillment? And that takes a little more work."

"Have you reached 'fulfillment' yet?" Fish challenged.

"This," said Sam calmly, "isn't about me."

*Huh. Where have I heard that before?* wondered Fish. "But let's talk about you. Sarah is worried about you, I think."

"I'm as I should be. She shouldn't worry. But," he

shrugged, "we should probably find you another coach sooner rather than later. I may not be here that much longer."

"What does that mean, exactly? Are you sick?" Fish peered closely at his friend.

Sam only shrugged. "Not sure yet," he said. "Probably nothing."

Leaving the office, Fish recognized he was feeling a bit let down. He really thought he had nailed it in executing his plan, but he realized that in the few months he'd been gone he'd only taken a couple of the steps he needed to take. He wished, at that moment, that he had started on this path a little earlier.

More than that, he was concerned about Sam. What he wasn't telling him. Where was he going, for instance? Was that illness talking? Or something else? He had left Sarah strict instructions to call him if there was anything ... any change ... in his friend.

She had agreed she would. But beyond the promise she didn't say anything. She acted like she couldn't.

# Chapter Twenty-Four

THE NEXT DAY Fish got up early with Ray. He planned a long run from the park through the town of Sisters a few miles down the road and back. He was always struck by Sisters' folksy charm. There was simply something about the funky place that attracted him. Soon enough they were running down the main streets, Ray stretching out and he glancing in the plate-glass store-front windows, looking for an unidentified something.

Unidentified until suddenly he saw the man. The man in his flash. The man Sam had drawn on the card. The one in his meditation vision. A tall man, thin to the point of almost being skeletal, almost a stick figure, depicted as a complex cartoon in the elaborately hand-drawn poster in the window of the art gallery. The walk, the bowl hat or hard hat, both distinctly similar to his vision.

Fish stopped, remembering the card, the last one Sam had given him. He carefully stared at every inch of the poster, noticing it had been affixed to the window with clear packing tape on the unpainted edges. He reexamined the drawing, read the description. No question it could be a match. And the type of person this was might (or might not) be someone Sam would recommend.

In reexamining the poster Jon realized something else. This was a very elaborate poster, hand done. Obviously not lithographed or copied, at least Jon didn't think so. How long would it have taken an experienced artist to draw this poster? Many hours, he thought. That made the odds good that this was the only poster made for this event. If that was true, why had it been hung along the one route he took in Sisters? Was Sam behind this? If not him, who? And why?

The possibilities of this event being useful for him were high, in any event. The description indicated that it was possible for Fish to determine his perfect path, and that The Good Reverend Rafael Aguilar was just the person to help him find that path, and that the Good Reverend Rafael could be found this coming Sunday at the Pentecostal Church in Bend. 2:30 in the afternoon, BBQ to follow. Children welcome. And dogs. $20 per person included all the BBQ you could eat, all the bones your dog could eat, and gospel music. Bring one question on a 3x5 card … if drawn, your life-question would be explored and answered, no extra charge.

Too cool for school! Fish had never heard of Reverend Rafael and definitely had never before seen dogs invited to church, but this was an event that Fish was not going to miss. He was intrigued by the 'all the bones your dog can eat' comment as well. Ray wasn't gonna get more than about one bone maximum, as bones and boxers don't always agree, but he knew some dogs could eat bones until the cows came home. Changed their attitudes, too. He remembered a black Lab he'd had as a kid. Rocky followed him around like they were glued together, but a bone made them two separate animals and even Fish wouldn't come between Rocky and a meaty beef knuckle.

Fish smiled to himself at the memory of Rocky, who he hadn't thought of in a while. Not since Ray came on board, anyway. But it isn't cheating to love one thing and cherish another's memory, is it? He didn't think so. Anyway, he was talking dogs here, not people.

A thought floated in: *When have I last missed a person?* And thought of Aardvark.

Sunday dawned as another perfect Bend day. Fish stretched out in the crisp early morning air, trying to find a gentle way to move so the Sun Salutation series of yoga poses wouldn't hurt too much. Pain doesn't equal gain with yoga, he had found. He gradually moved into the series, following the path, enjoying his practice. Ray was nearby, rubbing his back on the grass, doing his own stretches. A very good morning.

Fish didn't have a lot to do. He had run maybe too long with Ray the evening before. Had pickled himself out that previous morning. Sundays were more family time on the pickleball courts in Bend, anyway, not so much good play available. His parents were still cruising off-shore spending his inheritance. He didn't have any friends to check on. Was up to date on his journal. Other than going to the Reverend Aquilar's service in the afternoon, nothing called to him.

It was at times like this that Sam had advised Fish to just sit, meditate, and see what came up in the middle of nothingness. To demonstrate how it could be done in a real day, Sam recounted the story of meeting an old gentleman one day at a vegetable stand off Highway 27 in Bend. The old fella owned the stand, but this particular day was sitting on an apple crate when Sam had come in, hoping for some good tomatoes.

"He was looking into space. If he had been a Buddhist monk, I might have thought he was looking into some middle kingdom someplace. He wasn't sleeping, not day-dreaming, just present with some other inner reality. This guy, however, obviously grew tomatoes and probably wasn't a monk."

"Did you talk to him?" asked Jon, mildly curious.

"Sure, of course. I asked him why he was just sitting, in fact."

"What did he say?"

"He said 'I don't have nothin' to do, so I ain't doin' nothin'!'"

Jon had grinned and filed the story ... when you don't have anything to do, just don't do nothin' at all. Jon sat on the camp bench, braced his back against the table, and, doing nothing at all, without effort, followed his breath down and down.

Jon had experienced some moments in his meditation when he was one, not necessarily one with everything, but simply less fragmented at least, his monkey-mind more or less at peace, able to almost not think, or at least to hold one very small thought — like acknowledging the feeling of breath — without intrusion. Today, he was able to get there quickly, certainly more quickly than ever before.

This was a good thing in his practice, he had found, to be able to rejoin the furthest point he had experienced, whether within a yoga stretch or a meditation. Once he was there, he was familiar with it, felt no conscious reason to remain there and explore, but instead could relax into the next step, whatever that was.

Today the feeling of one-ness, or of whole-ness, felt very ... what ... solid? Real, in any event. He touched that, let it go, sank into it. His breathing slowed and slowed. At some very primitive level he realized he was scarcely employing any breath at all but felt nothing uncomfortable.

It isn't unusual for people who practice meditation regularly to occasionally find themselves in some altered state. But in fact that's often considered a disadvantage if it's seen as a goal. An extreme example would be levitation. Some who practice meditation go into it with a desire, a grasping to experience a different physical state like levitation or flying. Paradoxically, the desire to achieve any particular end will generally prevent the practitioner from achieving it. And Fish knew this, so he seldom looked for anything in particular besides the wholeness that, when it arrived, seemed very natural to him.

Today, however, another state superimposed itself on his meditation. Slowly but surely he found that he was in a place of illumination, a place bathed with a warm, golden glow. There was little in the place except for a small tree, a very ordinary elm, except with golden leaves. The tree floated with its roots trailing about it. All around the tree the warmth took on a slightly deeper dimension, like a golden fog becoming thicker on the tree's edges, outlining it someplace.

And just as he perceived this, he had an inner flash and he saw the tree disappear, leaving behind the golden fog outline. From within the outline, out stepped a stick figure. Once again he thought of it as a man doing the 'keep on truckin' walk, big foot forward, body back, tilting his body backward, tipping his bowler hat in Jon's direction. The aura floated toward the man, surrounding him and causing him to glow as had the tree. Jon remembered something about this particular aura. He had seen it recently.

Ever so slowly, the figure stepped back and the tree reappeared. In what seemed to be a predestined, natural order of things, the golden aura around the man floated out to surround the tree. A voice came from somewhere, a totally unique experience for Jon in this rare state, but still not one that made him uncomfortable. The voice was part of the golden aura. It was part of the tree, the man. Soon thereafter Jon floated up from the meditation and awoke, but he couldn't remember the words he had heard. The feeling he had was of profound relaxation coupled with an increased energy that wasn't at all jittery, but rather, was associated with a new energy. He knew he could do anything he needed to do at this moment. Likewise, he realized he didn't have any need to do any of those things. The experience had come and now it had gone. There was no imperative to take action, but certainly he could have.

Jon spent a long time writing down what he had experienced. As with dreams, it was common for him to lose most all the details of a meditation experience after a practice. But he didn't want to lose the details of this one, even though the experience faded somewhat even as he wrote in his beautiful journal.

Sometimes when he journaled he experienced almost a stream-of-consciousness effect that gave him some direction when later he reread his entries. But at this moment he didn't have that, except the memory of the voice came to him with one word he could remember and write down. He remembered it now perhaps because it had been repeated once, seemingly for emphasis.

"Share!" and in a moment "Share!" He wrote that word down. And the dream was gone.

Late in the morning Jon and Ray took another run through Sisters. Jon felt they both needed at least a small run after all and he had an ulterior motive. He wanted a last look at the poster.

When they arrived at the art gallery where the poster had been hung, it was gone. Jon supposed that it had been removed now that the day of the meeting had arrived. He looked carefully at the window. Whoever had removed it had done an excellent job of also removing the clear packing tape that had affixed the poster to the glass. It looked for all the world as if it had never been there.

## Chapter Twenty-Five

THE PENTECOSTAL CHURCH in Bend is a small church sitting on a pretty, wooded parcel of land off Highway 20. It's been there a while; it was there before Jon was born, he was sure. But it's not the oldest church in town. For that matter, it's not the smallest, either. Or, really, the prettiest. It is middle of the road in every sense, except for its congregation, who are very devout, given to evangelical outbursts not only in service but, occasionally, when proselytizing the faith on the street. Jon had seen several of them burst into tongues one time at a First-Friday Feed on Broadway Street, neither the type of thing Jon associated with Pentecostals nor the type of outburst normally seen on Broadway.

Having seen what he had seen he was not surprised that they would have this rather unorthodox sounding preacher in for what Jon thought of as a revival meeting. And certainly the idea of food and music accompanying any meeting at all was as natural to this group as breathing, so no surprise there. But when he arrived, early, he was surprised to find that dozens, maybe even a hundred people were already filling all the seats on the lawn in front of the church. He noticed a huge outside monitor and speakers, as if the event would be simulcast outside, and considered joining them with Ray on the lawn, but at the last moment decided to be inside to get the full flavor of whatever the Reverend had to offer.

Ray, too, seemed to want to be inside, pulling toward a

vacant seat in the third row. When they got there Jon realized Ray was only intrigued by the standard poodle also sitting in the pew next to them. Both dogs were content to sniff each other over politely so Jon moved into the last seat in the pew. The dogs sat next to each other, facing forward expectantly as if something was soon to be revealed for their ears alone. Jon stood and looked around. In addition to every seat now being filled and every extra seat in the upper choir area filled, people stood around the entire perimeter of the church. The number of dogs was considerable, some in every pew he could see. The choir was in full force in dark blue robes. Jon was hoping for great gospel music.

He remembered that this was the first time in several years he had attended a Christian church for any reason. Ironic that it took the combination of a personal revelation, gospel music, barbeque, and dogs to get him here. And here, inside, it was a remarkable place. He turned and studied the interior more closely. Outside a tidy but unadorned place, inside the church was spectacular, a lovely combination of whites, near whites, and soft golds, every available wood surface in the older church painted and gilded. The floors were worn warm brick, something he had never seen before in a modern church, reminding him of an old California mission. The huge ceiling-hung front altar cross supported a huge, thrice life-size replica of the Christ, with statues of saints in every niche.

This last was a real shock; Jon knew he was no expert but remembered that few if any Protestant churches memorialized the saints with statues, this being something that was usually left to the Catholics. In addition, there was a prominent statue of the Virgin Mary, again something he didn't expect at all to see. And she seemed Hispanic, which was cool with him but again, very unexpected indeed. Even the bench seats were unique, very comfortable and over-plush purple, and the kneelers were purple leather. Pretty nice, he thought, in a baroque kind of way.

He checked his watch; still fifteen minutes early but the buzz in the church was rising. The choir, which had been running through warm-up exercises, now moved gently into a very, very soft "Amazing Grace." Fish turned again. As Bend is, the choir seemed a mixed bag. The soloist now was a stunning redheaded woman, maybe forty-years-old. Fish flashed on her green eyes, although at this distance that was more a guess. He also guessed her as a soprano, although her throaty voice was singing an alto line in counterpoint to the other twenty-plus choir members. Fish took another look at her. She seemed familiar to him somehow. And given the lighting, she had an aura about her. No, she had that aura, the same thing he'd noticed with Aardvark when he first saw him in Palm Creek.

He turned to fully appreciate her and the choir when they began to sing, "We Are Here for You," and figured this classic opening song prefaced the appearance of The Good Reverend Rafael.

The master of ceremonies for this event was someone he knew slightly, having seen him around both the pickleball courts and Bend Parks and Recreation where Bill also worked. He was a hard-looking man, a bit younger than Fish, angular with only a rounded face softening the angles, a bit grizzled, with pale blue-grey eyes, looking like a younger Paul Newman when he smiled.

Bill looked around the room, giving this person and that a wink or nod or wave. He raised his eyebrows at Jon and smiled. *What are you doing here?* Fish imagined him asking.

Bill walked up the few steps onto the built-up podium, which held a straight-backed oak chair, a small table holding a rose-colored glass and pitcher, and a wireless microphone. "How many of you have heard of the Good Reverend Rafael?" he asked. Jon glanced around; certainly the majority of the audience had. "For those of you who have not, know you're in for a treat." And without any further ado he nodded to the back stage left, and walked off, leaving the stage empty.

The stage remained empty but somehow every dog in the place became energized at the same time, expressing it in various ways. Some, like Ray, began a low whiney keening that he only did when he really wanted something, like his ball stuck under the couch. The poodle turned around and stood on the backrest of the pew, as if searching for something at the entrance. The blonde, long-haired terrier two pews closer to the front began pawing at the air, while the corgi across the aisle hopped off its end seat and began turning quick circles in the aisle as if chasing its near-missing tail. Jon was fascinated by this, struck by the simultaneous action and by the fact that none of the dogs really verbalized. Nary one bark.

This went on for perhaps half a minute, during which time some of the dogs changed positions, others kept on doing what they were doing. Ray did both, laying down and curling up but continuing the low keening, a mix of behaviors Jon had never seen his young dog exhibit together.

Then all dogs became quiet once again and every dog Jon could see was now facing front, somber-faced, as if waiting for something inevitable.

A man slowly walked onto the stage. A very tall, very thin man, dressed in a simple grey, long-sleeved shirt and jeans, typical Bend wear. Jon pulled the new card out of his top pocket and looked at him, comparing. They could be the same, the card drawing left enough to the imagination that any thin person could have been represented.

The difference lay in the walk. In the static drawing on the card, the body position had been featured. like the iconic character mad hippie genius Robert Crumb had drawn for Zap Comics in the 1960s. That had always been a favorite 'thing' of Jon's anyway, the very idea conveyed continuing on in the face of any difficulty. But this was not that person, at least this person did not have that walk.

The man walked slowly up the wide steps to the podium and over to the microphone. He paused, took out a handkerchief, and wiped the microphone. Then he wiped the stand below the mic, then he wiped the back of the chair sitting on the podium next to the microphone. Lastly, he whisked off the seat of the chair. He took the wireless microphone off the stand and sat down and smiled sweetly at the audience. From his seat several rows back, Jon had to notice how big The Good Reverend's teeth were and how thin his lips, stretched across the teeth like two rubber bands. His teeth actually enhanced a good-natured but skeletal appearance in the man as if he had died years before in a very good mood.

"Good afternoon," he said into the microphone. "I know you've probably figured it out, but I'm Raphael Aguilar. Nice to meet you!"

If anything, his smile became wider as he talked. Jon flashed on Alice in Wonderland and the Red Queen and the Cheshire Cat, although he couldn't remember if the Cheshire Cat had disappeared except for its smile, or was it the Queen? 'One pill makes you larger,' he remembered from Grace Slick and Jefferson Airplane.

The Good Reverend continued. "Would you mind if I asked a few dogs up here on the podium with me?" he asked. "Dogs make me feel more comfortable."

Taking the good-natured smiles and nods as a global affirmative, he said, "For now, I'm gonna call up the dogs in the first three rows over … here. That's about a dozen, looks like. That's all I can hold up here." He pointed at the area where Jon sat. Ray would be one of the dogs if the man could pull this off.

Jon could feel the rustle through the audience and hear the whispers. He was riveted to the man, probably for the same reasons. The Good Reverend had just said he could call some dogs, but not others. Jon didn't think that could be done. He looked down his own row. Two older ladies sitting down at the end looked like twins, bookended by a pair of identical Scotties. The two women were nattering with each other, their wrinkled faces no more than two inches apart, as if they were speaking by sharing one tongue. The Scotties stared fixedly on the Good Reverend.

The Reverend now looked out into the audience and raised his right hand. With the hand raised he gestured, "come," by waggling his outstretched fingers.

Ray, the poodle, and the two Scotties from Jon's row all sat at attention, then hopped down on the floor, edged past their owners, and walked politely in a single line toward the front. The corgi in the next row did the same. In fact, Jon noted, every dog in those three rows had come forward! The smaller dogs walked up the steps onto the stage while the larger dogs, Ray, his standard poodle friend, and a yellow and chocolate lab jumped. There were three steps between the stage and podium and each dog went directly to their seats so that they were evenly distributed. The only issue came from the two Scotties who somehow confused their space with two Cairn terriers. There was a little pushing and shoving, but no growling. In very short order four or five dogs were on each of the three steps, all laying down quietly and looking out at the audience.

Jon had never before felt the sensation of his jaw actually dropping, but he did now. His jaw came unhinged and he sat with his mouth open, looking at the dogs. He couldn't have been more surprised if aliens had landed and asked for him by name.

"I bet you wonder how I did that," said the Good Reverend.

*Understatement of all time*, Jon thought. *Wow.*

"It's easy," the Good Reverence said. "You do have to have an unshakable belief in your ability to do it, though." He continued. "Is there something in your life right now that you are trying to achieve?" He smiled his toothy grin. "If there isn't, your life feels perfect, but I know it doesn't ..." he paused ... "you are here."

Jon smiled. *I'm just here for the barbeque.*

The Reverend went further. "Although there are those of you who believe they are really here for the barbeque," he said happily.

Jon smiled again. *I like this guy.*

Fish hadn't gone to listen to all that many motivational speakers, but he certainly didn't think the Good Reverend was typical. If he was one at all. Raphael was more about puncturing delusions, about saying stuff that was so exactly right for at least Jon's life that he felt like he was with a very close member of his family, someone who knew all about the bad stuff Jon had done, the dark stuff he wouldn't reveal.

"Do you regret not having close relationships?" Raphael now said. "Do you regret not even having one close friend?"

The guy was spooky, but his good nature about his proclamations, plus the pauses between them, gave Jon a chance to reflect on his words. Yes, he did feel that he had not even one close friend. Acquaintances? Sure. Friends? Not so much. Somehow — and he knew this was weird — he felt closer to Raphael than he did to most of his so-called friends in Bend. He thought about having come back and not having anybody to call other than his shrink and his parents. He found he missed Aardvark more than he had even realized.

It was then, missing the Aard, that he realized there were things in common between Raphael and his partner. Strange things, like the Aard's ability to know what Jon was thinking and verbalize it non-judgmentally. And his way with dogs. Wasn't what Raphael doing with Ray, who was still lying dead-still on the second step of the podium, exactly what Aardvark had done with the dog the first time they had met? It was! And whatever it was, it was the same technique... or non-technique.

While the Reverend's clothing was different from the Aardvark's, it appeared to Jon that both men had identical gold earrings. Gold earrings are common among men in Bend, but the distinctive curl of the serpent over the hoop was something of a signature. And lastly there was the aura again. Aardvark's had come and gone and wasn't as definite a golden color as was this one, but Jon, who was starting to see auras as normal, thought that it could be colored just by the overall golden glow within the church itself.

Jon could almost hear Aardvark. *Pretty poor series of coincidences. Nothing to it.*

The time went fast. The Reverend had started about on time, around 2:30, and Jon looked at his watch when he began his wrap up ... almost 4:15. Several things had been remarkable about his presentation, but of all of them perhaps the most was that none of the dogs had given any indication of moving during the entire time. The Reverend finished by hoping everybody would join him for the barbeque, where perhaps he could answer a few more individual questions for people as well. "I can't get to all of you, but if you need to talk with me, let's give it a try," he said. "Don't be shy! And in the meantime ..." he raised his hand, cupped it to his ear.

"Just keep on truckin'," those who had seen Raphael before answered back. Jon, who was starting to rise, sat back down. That was Robert Crumb's line, the line that went under that drawing, the man with the long legs disproportionate to his body, his big feet facing his audience. The picture that was on his newest card.

With that Raphael raised his hands, again waving his fingers, but now in a 'go' fashion away from his body. As if they were connected by strings, the dogs got up and, single file, walked back to their rows, where they hopped up on the seats next to their owners. Ray seemed none the worse for the experience, licking Jon's hand when Jon scratched his chest.

## Chapter Twenty-Six

THE BARBEQUE WAS STANDARD FARE, which is to say, excellent. There were pork ribs that had been lovingly brined and slowly cooked until the meat was falling off the bone, baked beans, of course, and homemade potato salad, in addition to macaroni salad and green salad, garlic bread, sweet and regular iced tea. Jon walked the whole buffet line before he joined in, so he could decide what goodies his appetite would enjoy. As he walked back toward the beginning, he noticed the redhead from the choir nearing the start. He delayed a bit to come in right after her and grabbed a plate. Ray trotted hopefully up and sat just behind.

There was a bit of a backlog and he used the delay. "Didn't I meet you at the cinematographer's party?" he asked.

She turned and grinned at him. He had never seen such perfectly even and white teeth. "Who am I to blow against the wind?" she responded.

He had always thought that the cinematographer's party line was classic Paul Simon and a great pick-up line; he had always wanted to use it but had never tried it before. This time, it came out naturally. The fact that she responded with the next line in the song knocked him out. He grinned back, suddenly feeling good about everything. He especially liked the fact that this woman he didn't know had instantly heard him and seen him, as

Aardvark had. *This is fun*, he thought.

"I'm Fish," he said.

"Gabby," she said.

And minutes later, their plates full, they were sitting next to each other on a picnic bench. She also had a dog, a blonde, long-haired terrier mix of maybe twenty pounds. "I don't know what Jersey is," she said in response to Jon's question. "I don't care, either. He's a great dog!"

Jon knew what she meant. It was how he felt about Ray. He loved Ray unconditionally and thought he was a perfect dog. Jersey and Ray gave each other a casual once over, more interested in the possibility of a bone than company, it seemed.

Gabby's and Fish's conversation was animated. She loved the thought that he was retired and was out finding himself in the world. She was a professional singer, making her living singing back-up and doing studio work. She had graduated from OSU, like Fish, but ten years behind him. So she was 42, with an alert and curious mind, passionate about her own interests and possibilities and best of all, she seemed interested in him. She was perfect, and maybe perfect for him, if he ever was to have a significant other friend.

And the fact that she was beautiful didn't hurt. "I wouldn't normally ask this question," he said. "But do you know you are exceptionally good-looking?"

Gabby laughed. "Is that the question? Do I know how I look to others?" She took a minute to consider, pulled a few strands of her hair around to chew on. "At this stage of my life I'm willing to accept my looks as an unearned gift."

"Does somebody like me have a chance with someone like you?" OMG, he had actually asked what he really wanted to know! *Pretty awkward*, he thought as a silence ensued.

"Maybe," Gabby said after about an hour. "What are your politics?"

Jon laughed. "These days I try not to have any," he said. "If it would help, I could promise that I'd never talk about them."

Gabby grinned at him. In addition to having wonderful, white teeth, she had a tiny little gap between her two front teeth. Not much, sort of like a dimple. Endearing. *I'm in trouble,* he thought.

The Good Reverend was working the crowd efficiently and after about two full plates ... Gabby keeping up impressively with Jon, who was ravenous ... he sat down on her left and leaned toward them. "I'm Rafael Aguilar," he said. "And you are ...?"

"Fish," said Fish.

"In awe of that trick with the dogs," Gabby said. "How did you do that?"

"Not so much a trick as a power. But I learned I had it and how to use it from a friend of mine," he said. "He was my mentor, actually."

"Wait," said Fish. "Does he have an earring identical to yours?"

"I knew it!" said the Reverend. "As soon as I saw you, I knew it. You know Aardvark!"

Gabby, bewildered, turned to Jon. "You know an aardvark?"

"The Aardvark, more like," Fish said. "Most likely there's only one." He turned to the Reverend. "But how did you know I know him?"

"The aura," Raphael responded. "It's distinctive."

"Mine? I have an aura?" He had thought nothing would

surprise him at this point, but he was surprised.

"No. Your dog does. It usually starts with the dog."

Gabby and Fish both stared at Raphael. After a long moment he laughed. "Just kidding. You don't have an aura. Neither does your dog."

"What then," asked Fish?"

"He told me you would be here. And that you were tall. And that you guys played pickleball together," nodding toward Jon's blue T-shirt, which featured a string of animals evolving from a monkey up through a pickleball player, complete with paddle and ball.

"I haven't seen him for days," Jon declared. "He didn't even know I was coming. I just decided last Friday!"

"You play pickleball!" said Gabby. "So do I!" She smiled at him fondly. "I knew there was something I liked about you."

"So is that 'maybe' now a yes?" Fish asked.

"Maybe," she said, and the three of them laughed.

There were many questions to be asked and answered, and The Good Reverend still had the rest of the crowd to work. "Can we get together after this is over?" he asked.

"Not for dinner," Jon said, puffing his cheeks out and making a fake-belching sound. "I won't be able to eat until Wednesday."

"Drinks at my place?" asked Gabby. "You better bring Ray, too." She glanced over at the two dogs, each with their current bone tucked under a paw, sleeping side by side like odd litter-mates.

"If I can wake him up," said Jon.

Gabby lived in one of the small employee shacks down on River Road, below the second town bridge over the Deschutes. Originally built for factory workers in the

lumber mills, the little houses, some on the river, were the
darlings of the city's growing real estate revival. Almost
worthless when built, any one of them would sell now for
a half million or more. Hers was a block away from the
river but was particularly charming, painted a vibrant blue
with white trim and a dark-gray roof, sparse landscaping,
gravel all raked like a Japanese garden, everything in
seemingly perfect repair. Jon and Ray got to the porch to
find the door open, with only the screen closed.

"Come in," said Gabby to his knock.

"Deal's off," said Fish as he and Ray walked into a
meticulous tiny living room and through to the yellow sun
porch where Gabby and Raphael sat.

"What deal?" asked Gabby.

"I can't date you. You're way too neat!"

"Army brat," she said. "I can make a bed you can bounce
a quarter off."

Raphael was sitting in one of the two wicker armchairs.
He looked very comfortable, although he had changed
shirts to a close-fitting blue T-shirt with a rising sun logo
on the front, which emphasized his extreme thinness.

"You know," Raphael said, looking down at his well-worn
flip-flops, "I had offered to answer questions for the
audience."

"How many questions did you get?" asked Gabby. "I
have a couple I forgot to ask."

"You're an exception, then. I seldom get any. People say
they want to hear about troubling aspects of their lives,
but really they don't."

Jon raised an eyebrow. "What makes you the expert on
other people's lives?"

Raphael seemed willing to take the snippy remark

seriously. "It's another power. I can answer life questions pretty well for some people," he said. "I arrived at it, but as I have gotten older it's become sharper."

"Problem is," he continued, "even when they do ask a question, they don't ask the question they really want answered. So my answers seem ... I don't know ... sort of problematic for some."

"Example?" asked Gabby.

"Well, one of the few questions I received yesterday was from a morbidly obese man who was trying to lose weight."

"And he wanted to know how?" she asked.

"He said that's what he wanted," he replied. "But that wasn't really it. As usual."

"I'll bite," said Jon. "What did he want?"

"He had been married for many years. But now he wanted to know if he had to lose weight to keep his wife."

"And you said ..."

"That he didn't have to."

"So, you told him that his marriage was okay ..." Gabby interjected.

"Well, it is what it is. I know his wife loves him, fat or thin. Problem is, she's very ill and I don't think either of them knows it."

Gabby and Jon tripped over each other with more questions. "How ill?" asked Gabby.

"Was she there?" Jon chimed in. "What did you say?"

"I answered his question ... he didn't have to lose weight, at least not now. She was there and I could see she's very sick. Pancreatic cancer level sick, something like that. She suspects, but they don't know, not for sure. He'll soon have bigger things to worry about than his weight."

"How did he take your answer?" Jon asked.

"He was confused. He had asked how to lose weight and I said he didn't need to at that moment. Not an answer he could understand, given that he's at least 100 pounds overweight."

"Does everyone ask the wrong question?" Fish asked.

"Usually yes, if they ask anything at all. Like I said, most people don't even ask." Raphael sank back into the cushions, seemingly becoming smaller. "Makes me sad," he said.

"How so?" asked Gabby.

"I want to be of service and I think I can be." He thought for a second, a finger at his thin lips. "Probably a different kind of service than people are ready for, though."

Jon thought that an ability like that would certainly give new definition to the term 'life coach.' "What do you know about me?" he asked. "What can you see that I should know about?"

"You're going to have a big year," Raphael said promptly. "Good and bad."

"How about my reaching my goals?"

"Irrelevant," said Raphael. "And you already suspect that. And your plan isn't directing you toward what you really want."

"That's crazy," said Jon. "I've got a whole plan worked out, and even my therapist agrees it hits my hot buttons." He thought about it. "I think he agrees, anyway."

"Better check again," Raphael said, a slight smile tugging up the corners of his mouth.

Gabby laughed. "Planning; I tried that once. I didn't like it. I don't do plans anymore."

Raphael looked at her. "And you," he said to her, quite seriously. "You've got a lot of gumption. But you've held yourself back 'til now. Now you're finally willing to truly commit to something."

"I sort of get that," she said pensively. "I imagine if something does come along worthy of committing myself to, I could do it."

"Actually, I meant right now," said Raphael. "There is something in you that wants to make a commitment right now, this minute, today."

Jon and Gabby stared at Raphael as if he had grown a third eye. And you wonder why nobody asks you anything," said Jon finally.

"I don't know of anything right now," said Gabby.

"Really?" Raphael looked over at Gabby and raised an eyebrow.

"Oh," she said in a small voice, glancing briefly at Fish. "I see."

Fish, for once in his unaware life, noticed Gabby's glance. This made him feel very shy, almost timid, somehow. But he also felt ... he didn't know the word ... blessed? Was that too much? Yes, it was too much, he decided. But it was certainly new and nice.

Remembering his earlier comment about neatness, she looked directly at him. "Just how messy are you?" she asked.

Jon noticed her eyes. Very nice eyes. Brown flecks on green. Pretty terrific with the freckles and red hair and all. "'Bout average, I'd say. I pick up underwear every few days. Wash dishes when the sink is full. Like that."

"Oh, poo," she said.

"Listen, Fish," said Raphael, ignoring their side

conversation, "I didn't mean you aren't moving toward what you need. You are. What did Sam actually tell you?"

"You know Sam, too? This is way too weird. How do you know him?"

"When Aardvark came to help me recently, he told me a lot about you. Including who your therapist is since we both know him anyway."

The pieces began to fall into place. "You're the one he left camping with me to go help?"

Raphael nodded. "Um-hm. Took him a couple of days to get my head out of my rear. Worse than usual, that episode."

Gabby laughed. "I never thought about actually trying to help somebody else do that," she said. "Terrible mental picture."

"I can answer other people's questions," Raphael said, ignoring their side comments again, "but usually not my own."

"So you use the Aardvark ..."

Raphael smiled. "That's what the Aardvark does," he said. "He roots around ..."

"Like an aardvark," Jon said, understanding, finally.

"Yep, you've got it. Like an aardvark. Until he finds what we need to see. Then he brings it out into the open. Suspect he's already done that with you." He pointed a thin index finger Jon's way. "He's been working on the external stuff with you, he says."

Flash. "Oh, I get it!" Jon exclaimed. "External and internal stuff." He remembered that was what Sam had told him in the parking lot. And it was true. Much of what Aardvark had worked on with him had been external stuff. His serve, for instance. A bunch of stuff. But not the internal stuff; feelings, awareness, his own sense of power in a difficult world ... not so much.

"Why wasn't he working on my internal stuff, if he's so good?" Jon asked.

"Yeah. He could have saved me some effort," Gabby muttered, thinking again about cleanliness and her neat-as-a-pin life.

Raphael grinned at them. "One thing at a time. The Aard won't give you more than you can use. External is easier at first."

"Okay, so he's like ... everybody's mentor? Or anybody's?" asked Gabby. "And you're what ... their Oracle?"

"Definitely he's not everybody's mentor. He's selective." He thought about it. "And this thing with answering questions, it's a power. It developed into full form only when I arrived."

"Arrived?" asked Gabby.

"Hard to explain," said Raphael. "Think of it as coming into your full being. Not like 'enlightenment,' which few people achieve. Anybody can arrive, if they work at it."

"What kind of things does he look for?" asked Jon. "Why'd he take me on?"

Raphael answered their questions with a question. "Did you ever observe him? I mean, really, really watch him closely? Like you were studying a complicated diagram in a book?"

Jon thought back to the very first time he had seen him. "Yeah!" he said. "I did. And he even complimented me on how well I was watching him."

Raphael nodded knowingly. "How does he greet you now?"

"Oh!" Jon said. "We greet each other the same way, usually. 'I see you, Aardvark.' And 'I see you, Jon.'"

"What does that tell you?"

Gabby interjected. "He puts a value on seeing who someone really is," she said. "I'm right, aren't I?"

"Yeah, but it's more than that. It's his being seen as well. And the effort a person puts into the seeing," Raphael said. "Some people never really see another person at all, not truly."

"Is this going to help my pickleball game?" Jon couldn't help himself. "Improving my game is part of my plan, you know." He looked at them sideways.

Gabby stared at him like he had just eaten a worm. "Pretty dumb plan, if you ask me. Pickleball is just a game, not a metaphor for life."

"Actually, do you remember my asking your opinion?" Jon asked sarcastically. "Neither do I."

"Clever. Did you get that off a tee-shirt?" Gabby asked.

Raphael looked at them fondly. "Now, children," he said.

"Did we just have our first fight?" asked Gabby.

"Did I win?" asked Fish.

# Chapter Twenty-Seven

TUESDAY WAS the best pickleball day at Pine Nursery Park. All the local 4.0s and above who didn't have to work showed up. The four courts set aside for non-club members were full as well. As expected with the upcoming regional tournament, there was a great showing, all skill levels. Gabby and Fish were playing against Aardvark and Kirk, his former partner who had developed plenty of chops.

Aardvark and Kirk began by taking it easy on Gabby, concentrating mostly on Fish, but as the game progressed, it was clear that Gabby could keep up. Mostly she softened hard shots and played at the net, but was very capable of hitting a ball hard. When she did she most often went right at the other two, something that Fish, in his experience, had not seen women do that regularly.

Aardvark spent the whole game with a huge smile, watching Jon very closely. Something has changed, Jon thought. He actually knew something had; something had shifted inside him. It wasn't just Gabby, although she was a huge part of this. It was more that for the first time, he felt nearly present, a participant in his own life instead of being merely a spectator. This was an odd experience, but not entirely unfamiliar. He had had flashes of it recently, he remembered. When he first met Aardvark at Palm Creek, for instance. Other times, too; the game where he had been in the zone at the Thousand Trails tournament was another.

Gabby, he realized, was the best woman player he had ever played with. And he was beginning to think that she was pretty cool in other ways as well. He wasn't that experienced with having a girlfriend. Closest was a brief infatuation that had quickly morphed into a cordial but loveless marriage. With Gabby, some of it was challenging, but some of it felt like coming home, like falling off a log. It was that easy, except when they fought, which apparently was going to be the regular order of things on the pickleball court.

He smiled. It wasn't so bad, having someone to fight with, he thought. He could see how couples stayed together a long time. It would take that long, he thought, to really work through some of his stuff.

One goal in his plan to become the best pickleball player he could had receded so far into the background he simply didn't think about it. As the Good Reverend said, the plan itself had become irrelevant. He knew at almost a cellular level that he was acting in the manner the universe wanted him to act. And he was pretty sure he wasn't only talking about pickleball.

## Chapter Twenty-Eight

THAT EVENING, Aard and Fish went out to their camp chairs at the edge of the little lake in the Bend-Sisters RV Park. They were staying at the park until the Bend tournament was over, still ten days out, and they had settled in. It was several days since the BBQ and a couple since the Aard and Gabby, Kirk and he had lit up the court together. Soon after the match, the Aardvark had pulled another disappearing act and was off. Fish imagined he was helping another of his circle of seekers to apply Right Thinking and Right Action, metaphorically pulling another head out of another rectum somewhere in the region. But he was back now.

"How many folks do you work with?" asked Jon.

"The group? A couple of dozen, I'd guess. But only when they need something. Some of them go years between." The Aard was cutting his amazingly thick fingernails with the largest nail clipper Jon had ever seen and shaking the cuttings off into the lake, where a school of small fish was swarming them.

"How come you spend so much time with me, then?" Jon asked.

"Not what you really want to know again, Jon-Boy." Fish shook his head. "Slow learner, you."

"No, it really is what I want to know," Jon said. "You are very good for me, Aard, and I thank you. You are my friend, and you know I don't say it lightly."

"You just answered your own question, Fish." Aard reached over and held Jon's shoulder for a moment. "I spend time with you because you are my friend. Some of the others are ... something else."

"Customers? Disciples? Fans?"

"It's more like they are a necessary resource I learn from," said Aardvark. "That's you, too, but you are also my friend. It's complicated."

"Speaking of learning, did I ever ask you what you can do?" Fish considered. "Beyond what you've shown me, I mean."

"Parlor tricks? I can do lots of them, if that's what you want to see."

"It's alright for an off-night," Jon said.

"In a kind of limited way," Aard sang.

"Did you know that Gabby can do that, too?" Jon scrunched his chair sideways on the dirt to face Aardvark more directly.

"Finish Paul Simon song lyrics? Lots of people can do that, Jon. Don't make too much of it."

"See, you're always doing that. I'll be impressed with something I do, or someone else does, or some coincidence, or something. And you'll say, 'don't make too much of it.'"

"Well, am I wrong? Should you be making more of those things? Think about it in terms of fifteens."

"Fifteens?"

"Yeah. Would this have mattered fifteen minutes ago? Fifteen seconds ago? Can you assume you would care about this fifteen days from right now?"

Jon thought about that for a long time. "Is this some kind of Koen? A new version of 'the sound of one hand clapping' or something?"

"I don't do Koens. They're ridiculous. They pose questions that nobody would care about to begin with and then people expect that they'll experience enlightenment when the top of their head blows off trying to figure the answer. Might as well just beat themselves on the head with a hammer and expect enlightenment when they stop."

"That would be the longest paragraph I ever heard you say," Jon said.

"And I shouldn't have said any of it," said Aardvark. He picked up a flat rock and skimmed it, skipping it maybe four or five times, creating a line of rings across the pond. "How long will those rings last? How high is up? Who cares?"

Jon thought about it, picked up another rock, leaned and aimed and tried to skip it along the same path his friend had followed. "Nobody would care about that, I guess," he admitted.

"And, see, that's the point, grasshoppah. People should care less about things. They should observe without caring, without attachment. Taking action without attachment is almost always Right Action, I think."

"So, when I make an awful serve …"

"Which you seldom do any more …"

"Which I seldom do," Jon agreed. "Then it doesn't matter, in terms of the fifteens? And if I let it go completely it will lose its hold on me?"

"And," the Aardvark continued, "you can come to it and appreciate it as just another thing that's come and gone, no more likely to have an impact on your next serve or any next serve than the proverbial tree falling in the forest has on the sound it makes …"

"… if no one is hearing," Jon finished. "I get it. But how do I do it?"

"You don't," said Aard. "That's the whole trick of it. The minute you try to do it, it slips through your fingers like mercury slides from a broken thermometer. You can't hold onto anything. And if you try, then you fail."

As the evening deepened Ray snurfled around the edges of the pond trying to scare up a frog. "Watch Ray," said Aard. "Mostly dogs live in the moment. They do suffer once we get them fully domesticated so they depend on us. But left to their own devices, they could live, procreate, die all in the moment. And we say they are subordinate to us, lower mammals."

"I certainly don't say that," said Fish. "Who cleans up whose poop?" He leveraged his tall body out of the chair, took a poop bag out of his pocket, and walked over to the mound Ray had deposited next to the pond's edge.

"Apropos of nothing," said Aardvark, "how is your eye?"

After a moment of poop collection Fish came over and bent down to look Aardvark in the face. This was difficult to do because of his height and because Aard was sitting so deep in the chair. "It's pretty dark, but you know, if I put my hand over my right eye, I think I can see you! Is that possible?"

"When did you think about it last?"

"The injury? Months, maybe. A long time."

"Then," said the Aard, "yes, I think it's possible you have regained at least some sight in that eye. I thought you had, just by the way you looked at the path of circles when I threw that rock on a few minutes ago. You bent down and sighted with your left eye. Not your right."

"I find it hard to believe I wouldn't have noticed before this." Jon now walked around with his hand over his right eye, navigating pretty well in the twilight, *thank you very much*. He was surprised how pleased he was, although truth be known, he was only recognizing something that apparently had been there for some time.

"Do you think about the plan?" Aardvark asked.

"Funny you should ask. Gabby and I had a discussion about that recently with Raphael. He said the plan was irrelevant."

"What did Gabby say?"

"She gave me the 'planning is dumb' line, is all."

Aardvark looked pensive, Jon thought, at least what he could see of him through his recently blind left eye. "What are you thinking?" he asked the shorter man.

Aardvark looked at a joint that had magically appeared, lit, in his hand and took a hit. "She's a good one," he said.

"I know," Jon said. "I know." He took the offered joint, took a hit, handed it back.

"Don't screw it up," said Aardvark.

"I know," said Jon, and they both laughed.

# Chapter Twenty-Nine

THE NEXT DAY Fish went to see Sam. Sarah was wearing pink, a good color for her. "You look nice," Fish smiled. She smiled back, obviously pleased he had noticed. "But he's not here, is he?" Fish said.

"Nope, he's …"

"Ten minutes out, and said I should go in and get comfortable?"

"Huh. Psychic," said Sarah. "And he left something for you."

Fish expected to see another 3x5 card laying on his chair. He was half right. This time there were two cards. He picked them up and shuffled them in his large hands before looking at either.

The first picture was pretty simple. No people, but a moon or sun in the sky, a plain landscape below containing nothing but a tree, a simple one, like a child's drawing of a pine tree. The second was more complex with a couple of intertwined figure eights, or they could have been snakes. This card reminded Fish of the earrings Raphael and Aardvark wore, except it was a real stretch to make earrings out of the figures. But maybe. The only thing he'd learned from the cards thus far is that they had meaning, and usually (based on the sample of his previous two) involved a person he would meet. The other thing in common was that both people knew Sam from some other part of his life; perhaps they knew his son, as the Aardvark had said, but maybe that was just incidental. He tucked both cards in his pocket as his therapist clopped into the room.

The noise tipped him off and he turned; Sam was wearing a leg cast. "What the hell did you do?" Fish asked.

"Almost nothing," Sam said grumpily. "Tripped over a chair. Wound up in emergency. Fractured two bones in my foot. Did you know there are twenty-six bones in your foot? So I broke about eight percent of them."

"Are you all right? Is there anything I can do?"

"No, and no. But I'm back at work, slaving over a hot notepad. Not that you care." Sam slumped down into his chair, putting his leg straight out in front of him at the side of his desk. "Have I mentioned that I hate being laid up like this? And I can't get comfortable wearing this cast."

"Don't take it out on me," Fish protested. "I didn't do it."

"Yeah, well ... how are you, anyway?"

"Like you don't know. You've been tracking me like a drone."

"What are you talking about?"

"Both the Aardvark and Raphael Aguilar seem to know a lot more about me than they should. Haven't you heard of patient confidentiality?"

Sam got a little red in the face. "I didn't tell either one of those guys anything from our meetings," he said. "In my own defense you may have noticed that both of them are simply more perceptive than average."

Jon had to admit that was true but wasn't going to let Sam off the hook. He waved his hand dismissively. "No matter," he said. "I'm sure you had your reasons for airing my dirty laundry in their presence."

"Well," Sam said, "if I had done it, I would think it was for your own good. Anyway, it sounds like things are coming together for you."

"See? See what I mean? What do you know already, before I tell you?"

"Hey, I don't know that much. Anyway, Sarah is part of this. I have no idea how she finds out the stuff she does. But Bend's a small town and she's been here all her life. She told me most of what I know."

"In any case, you're right," Fish said. "Things have been working better in my life. Not the plan. The plan hasn't been working. But something is."

"How hard are you working at it?" Sam tapped his pencil pensively on his cast.

"The plan? I'm not working it at all these days. I just show up and life happens."

"Is that a Woody Allen line?"

"Don't think so. Might be John Lennon, actually. But it's true. Did you hear about Gabby?"

"Of course I did. Anyway, I know her father, Gus, and I've known her family forever. He had as good a voice as Sarah says Gabby does. He still lives here in Bend. Ex-military guy, Air Force. Full colonel when he mustered out, I think."

"She and I are dating." The words surprised him. They had a certain ring to them. Like finality, or a commitment.

"Un-huh. And how is your pickleball?"

"Interesting, but I don't care as much about being a top player as I did. As a result, I'm playing pretty darn well. I'm just not as ... attached to it as I was, I guess I'd say."

"Do I understand from that that you are doing less, but

getting more out of it?"

"Yeah. You know, I really enjoy playing the game now. I had started to lose that when I started setting goals for myself. I dropped the goals and found a game I had almost lost."

"You're on target, but you're wrong about the plan not working. The plan had its value. It got you jump-started. But I think there's even more for you out there than you think."

"Like what?"

"I could tell you, but ..."

"You'd have to shoot me. I know. And I'm supposed to discover these things for myself, aren't I?"

"You bet. You wouldn't believe them otherwise."

Jon was puzzled. "What do you mean?"

"Would you have ever believed me about the Aardvark? Who would? Or even about the Good Reverend, if I just told you they were going to be significant for you?"

"Probably not," Jon admitted grudgingly. "I suppose my investment in them led me to believe in them?"

"Something like that," Sam said. "But there's more out there. Quite a bit more. Go forth ..." he waggled his fingers in the direction of the parking lot ... "and prosper!"

Jon got up. "Hope your foot is better soon." He tucked the two new cards in his jacket pocket as he stood to leave. "Oh ... want to come to the car and say 'hey' to Ray?"

"Six weeks, minimum, before my foot heals, the doctor says," said Sam gloomily, winching himself upright. "Could have been worse, I guess."

~

Jon and Ray went back to camp and from there they took off for a longish run, he figured maybe seven-eight miles to Sisters and back. They passed the art studio where the poster for Raphael had been hung. On a hunch, Jon parked Ray in a sit outside the studio and stuck his head in. "Got a question," he said to the short, bespectacled young man wandering the studio with a clipboard, taking some kind of inventory.

"Shoot," the man said in a reedy voice.

"Do you remember that poster you had in the window? That one advertising Raphael?"

The man laughed. "That really isn't a poster. It's back here." He pointed to a spot on the wall toward the back. "You can bring your dog in if you want to look."

Ray and Jon walked the long, narrow space toward the back. Sure enough, the poster was hung on the wall, about the last one short of the bathroom. It had a price tag on it. $750. There was a tiny red label saying "sold" on the frame at the top.

"You're kidding. $750?" Jon was shocked.

The younger man didn't bat an eye. "Spectacular price, I think. Especially for an Aardvark!"

Jon wasn't sure he heard correctly. But as he looked closer, he saw a scrawled letter A in the lower left corner, along with the year. "You said Aardvark?"

"Sure. We're the only store in town to have his stuff, and this is the only one he gave us this year."

"Did you know," Jon asked, "that this picture actually advertised a real event?"

"It would," the other said. "He's sort of the ultimate realist, after all."

"Yeah? You could have fooled me. Who bought it?" he

asked.

"I wasn't here when it was sold."

"Could you look?" Jon found himself more curious about the buyer than about Aardvark's having drawn it.

"Privacy," the man said. "Can't do it."

*The guy is always interesting,* Jon thought. Ray and he spent another minute, staring, Ray seemingly as interested as he, before they left to continue their run.

That evening was another classic Bend summertime occasion. Few places in the world are as beautiful as Bend in the summer, and the evenings, to Fish, were the best part of the best days. He and Aardvark were again sitting at the edge of the campground's pond, and Ray was again off terrorizing the frog population.

"I didn't know you were an artist," Jon said. "Saw your poster-painting thing in the Quilt Shoppe gallery today."

"I dabble," said Aard. "I like fine work more. Jewelry. Like that."

"Did you know it sold?"

"Nope. They'll probably call me when they want to send a check."

"You aren't excited." Jon watched the rings as a large trout rose, just beyond casting distance, to a sporadic mayfly hatch.

"It's not in the moment for me. Once I finish a piece, it's gone. I try not to wonder about it."

Jon thought that was consistent. He changed subjects. "Last night you were gonna tell me about the things you can do. 'Parlor Tricks,' I think you called 'em."

"Was I? Usually I don't talk about them."

"You don't have to. I was just curious."

"No, I remember. It's okay. Let's see …" Aardvark slouched back in his chair. "There's telepathy. Some limited healing, like out-of-place joints and such. Real card magic …"

"Wait … that last …"

"Card magic?"

"Real card magic. As opposed to fake card magic?"

"Card work done by a stage magician is amazing, but it's still fake. Mine is real, with some caveats." He took a red deck of bicycle cards out of his pocket. "Want to see?"

"You were carrying a deck of cards? Were you expecting to show me that one?"

"Clairvoyance," he said. "That's one I forgot." He spread the cards slightly on the small folding drinks table between them. "Shuffle these."

Jon took the cards and shuffled them a dozen times. "Enough?" he asked.

"Sure. Now cut them a few times, then shuffle them some more." He waited.

"Now place them face down on this table and mix them all together," he said. "Then square them up." Aardvark was studiously keeping away from the table. He seemed to be staring off at the back corner of the campground.

"'K, done," said Fish.

"Now take the first four cards off the top and turn 'em over. Tell me what you find."

Jon took the top four cards off the top. And turned them over. "Whoa," he said. "Didn't expect that. Wait … do you know what I found?"

"Well, probably four aces. Could be four deuces, though."

"Wrong." Jon turned over four threes. "How did you do

that?"

"Sometimes the first set is wrong. That's the caveat. I can't always predict the first set exactly. But once I know the first set, I always know what the next sets will be."

"The next set? Fours?"

"Nope. Four Fives. It'll jump two each time, now. It should end with ... let's see ... aces."

Jon quickly riffled through the deck. Sure enough, each succeeding group of four cards was another four of a kind, starting next with fives, then sevens, nines, and so on, ending with deuces.

"You never touched those!" Jon said accusingly.

"Duh. Real magic, remember?" Aardvark said. "I could have been in my trailer and the outcome would be the same." He looked slyly at Jon. "Notice anything else?"

Jon looked at the cards for several seconds before he realized what he was looking at. "The cards were red, weren't they?" He rubbed the blue color on the back of one.

Aardvark smiled. "Yes, they were, weren't they?"

For some reason this impossible trick seemed just another implausible thing that the Aardvark could do. Jon was impressed but not shocked. "Can you teach me to do this stuff?" he asked.

"No point to it. You'll get your own powers when you are ready," Aardvark said. "I really can't teach them or even predict what you'll get."

"I'm gonna get powers?"

"Don't act so surprised. Yes. That goes with your arrival," Aardvark said.

"Arrival where?" Jon asked. Aardvark just stared at him and didn't answer.

"Where I'm going. Right?"

"Sarah is right," the A nodded. "You aren't just a pretty face!"

"How did you know she said that to me yesterday? Telepathy, I bet."

"She told me," Aardvark said with a toothy grin. "Anyway, you were looking for a word to discuss the group of us. Family works. Or circle. We're different souls united in a search for the One."

"I should know this …" Jon hesitated.

"One. One thing. One with self," the Aardvark hinted.

"You're patronizing me. You're talking about enlightenment, right?"

"Not in the sense people usually mean it. I'd rather call it Arrival. You arrive at yourself, you feel integrated, whole. You feel in the moment, a bit more present. But you aren't Siddhartha, the Buddha. You don't have to sit under the tree of enlightenment to arrive at yourself."

"So, you're enlightened," Jon stated, more fact than question. "Sorry, you've arrived!"

"Yeah, I did arrive a while ago. Well, quite a while. Maybe like twenty years ago."

"And your powers …"

"Most likely they all showed up at the same time, although it took a while for me to realize I had some of them. I mean, card magic isn't something anybody tries to do daily just to see if they've acquired the knack."

"You talk about them like they're ordinary."

"They are. Or at least they should be, Jon. Face it … the urban legend we work with is … what … that only five percent of our mind is engaged? Ten maximum, if you're a high-producing genius? Say that's true and we don't use

211

much of our own horsepower. Imagine what you would find you could do if you were able to operate at twenty percent? Thirty? Maybe you could do anything you wanted at that level. They've done movies around that concept, books have been written about it, but of course, nobody really knows completely."

"So the powers are already in each of us? Doesn't make sense. If we can have more, be more, why don't we?"

"How do you do it?" Aardvark replied. "You make it sound like, if we try, we can get there. But trying makes everything worse, not better. Think of your pickleball game. Your serve. Was it better when you tried harder?"

"Much worse," Jon said. "So, I'm interested. How do I arrive? What do I do next?"

"Next? There is no next. You just stay as awake as you can. Oh, and you can wear this, if you want." He handed Jon a small package. "Happy birthday."

"My birthday is two months off." Jon turned the box to look at its wrapping.

"Well, maybe I should have said Happy Beginnings instead. And welcome to the circle."

Inside was one earring, a gold hoop. A serpent crawled around its outside and was currently facing inward, flicking its golden tongue. Jon held it up. The eye of the serpent was a tiny ruby. The finish was antique, slightly dull, but the serpent's tail was brightly colored. It was, in every way, identical to the one Aardvark wore every day.

"It's beautiful! So you're the guy who made Raphael's and your own," Jon deduced.

"Uh-huh. I've made them all. Everybody in the group has one. Nobody has to wear them, of course. Sam doesn't, for instance."

"What does it do for us? Or you?" He worked the point

of the earring through the pierced hole in his left ear. He closed the clasp and felt the hoop, smooth and heavy.

"Pretty much nothing I know of," admitted the Aard. "But it does identify you as one of our family. I find I can use the family's help sometimes on the journey."

"You know, about that journey thing … I could just hang with you," said Jon. "I know I must be getting older but at this point I'd rather just hang."

"That's part of your journey. Not wanting to really go on a journey at all. But now that you've started, you won't stop."

"Until I arrive," Jon said. "Sounds like something Sam said."

"Oh, you mean about 'you can become more'?"

"Right! He told you?"

"No," said the Aardvark. "That one was telepathy."

By this time it was almost dark. Ray had scared up frogs all around the pond and now was back, laying at the Aard's feet. Jon could see the white blaze on the boxer's chest and that was about all. He was very content, a feeling which he didn't analyze. He just was.

Tomorrow would be another day. Maybe he would learn more about his future powers. Maybe his pickleball game would be magical again. Maybe neither, or something else entirely. He was fine with it all, for right now.

Over the next ten days Aardvark and Jon played pickleball several times. They had had their late-entry into the Bend Regional 4.0 confirmed by the tournament director, who also took a second to jab Fish a little. "So now that you've killed the little fish, you're gonna go fish in the Big Pond? Good luck with that!" Cheetah wrote in her confirming email.

"That's why they call me Fish," Jon wrote back, not being able to think of anything snappy. Realistically he didn't favor their chances either. Looking at the player list, he didn't see any easy way through. When he shared this with Aardvark, however, he got an entirely different, although perhaps (given what he was starting to know) it was a predictable reaction.

"Anything is possible," smiled Aardvark. "I feel pretty good about our chances, myself."

"Yeah, but you're the guy who played off-handed in Casa Grande just for the thrill of it," Fish groused. "I'd like to at least show up."

"That's more about you than the player list, isn't it? You're grasping again."

No arguing with that, Fish decided. Like arguing that the moon is or isn't made of green cheese. Arguing about a perception doesn't make the situation into a positive. He walked over to the picnic table behind the courts, where Ray was busy on his back, scratching himself in the grass. Ray's back legs were splayed out and his boxer tongue lolled back and forth.

"You're a piece of work," Fish said, kindly. Ray barely looked up.

## Chapter Thirty

FISH AND AARDVARK mostly practiced together, but occasionally one of them discovered something they wanted to experiment with and would play with other players to work on it. They were getting better and better as a team, though, and it was sometimes a disappointment to Jon whenever they split up. He could simply play better with the Aard than with anyone else, so why shouldn't he just do that?

And then there was Gabby. Gabby was an exception. He loved playing with her, and these days she was often around. In fact, she was almost a fixture, the third leg on the stool, the third Musketeer. Gabby and Fish did everything together except one. For some reason neither of them was pushing sleeping togther at all, although it was clear by their kissing and constant touching that the next logical step could be pretty magical. It seemed as if that next step wasn't ready to be taken, and so they didn't have to talk about it, although Jon thought about it. Being in love brought out his teenage tendencies and fantasies. He liked it.

Playing mixed doubles with Gabby was revealing. He found he could be as fond as fond can be with her off the court, while on court his behavior was terrible. Worse, she was able to catch him being irritated with her in a nanosecond. He could not face her all he wanted, but she could do an instant read on body language and whenever she made a mistake she was quite ready to light him up if

215

he criticized her. She didn't want for temper on the courts.

She was also quite ready to point out his errors. For instance, he thought he should be captain of the courts when he was playing with her. She disagreed. "You're not perfect," she pointed out. "You poach my sitters way more than you should!"

"I've got a very good poach," he huffed. "You should recognize that."

She looked at him. "Keep away from my forehand," she warned. "Or we're getting a pickleball divorce."

He started laughing but then stopped. "You're serious," he realized.

"Like a heart attack," she agreed, stalking back to her position.

## Chapter Thirty-One

"IT'S DIFFERENT playing pickleball with a woman," he said to Aardvark that evening. "She should let me play my strengths. She wants to be equal but she's really not, not on the pickleball court."

"'Equal' isn't the word you want. Her game is different from yours, but overall she's pretty darn good."

Fish didn't disagree but he wasn't going to admit it, so he changed the subject. "Wanted to ask more about your group," he said instead.

"Uh-huh," acknowledged Aard. "The Family."

"So … there's … mmm … how many of us?"

"A couple of dozen, more or less."

"How long have you been helping them? Or us?"

"Forever. Well, a couple of decades, anyway. I started with it right after my own 'Arrival'."

"And everybody has some special powers, yet we're all still struggling."

"Sure. Think of it as a list of lottery winners, which in a way you are. But say the list only contains those people who go broke after winning a lottery because they didn't have sound financial guidance. I'm that financial counselor. I help the family stay off that list."

Fish thought about that. It made sense. He fingered his new earring. "Am I supposed to do something with my powers when they show up? Something to help other folks, I mean?"

"Has anybody asked you for help?" Aardvark asked. "You don't help if they don't ask. It's their journey, not yours."

"I didn't ask you for help," Fish protested, his face getting warm.

"Yes, you did," Aardvark said. "Maybe you didn't know it at the time. It was when you asked if we could play together."

*Yeah, I remember,* he thought. "Do we have … like … meetings or anything?"

"Probably you'll never see more than a couple of us at any one time," said Aardvark. "And if it weren't for this — " he touched his own earring — "you might not even see those. We all lead pretty normal lives, more or less. We don't go around flying or bending spoons or …"

"… reading people's minds?"

"No, we do that one if we can. Who would know?"

Jon thought about the upcoming Bend tournament. "How much of this do you use when you play tournaments? Seems like it would give you an advantage."

"I choose not to use any of it. You have to work at it sometimes, but you can manage to keep your mental hands off."

"So in Bend …"

"… we'll get what we earn," Aardvark finished. "No parlor tricks."

Jon didn't know if he should be happy or sad about that news. It would be tempting to go in with an advantage. It wouldn't even be an unnatural advantage, not if everyone had the natural capability to achieve these powers. It'd just be using what was given you, such as using both hands if a person was truly naturally ambidextrous …

… which gave him a thought. He reached and took a large can of Arizona Iced Tea out of his cooler and quickly tossed it to Aardvark's left hand.

Aardvark caught it fluidly and put it down by his side. "Not yet, still workin'," he said, holding up his half-finished tea with his right hand.

"Were you born ambidextrous?" Jon asked. "I'm thinking you weren't."

"Why?"

"'Cuz when I first saw you playing left-handed in Casa Grande you stunk."

"Good observation. I wasn't born with it. It was part of the welcome package. The arrival gift. But I can turn it on or off. Usually I just leave it on unless I have a reason not to use it. Like I did there."

"That's pretty complicated," said Jon. "Brings up more questions …"

"… which I won't answer," said the Aard. "What we're dancing around is a code of ethics, sort of. We on this journey 'Arrive,' get talents, and should choose to use them responsibly. Not necessarily for the 'greater good,' but in an appropriate manner in whatever circumstances we're in."

*Shit*, thought Jon. *This is hard.* "So somehow I can play pickleball either responsibly or irresponsibly?"

"Sure. 'Irresponsible' would be using your powers so others were confused, misled, or damaged. Imagine choosing to win a pickleball game using talents or choosing not to use them and risk losing."

That was easy enough to see. The risk of losing also gave the opponents more opportunity to win. In turn he'd get their best game which helped him. He was struck with a memory of a biblical phrase. *To he in whom much is entrusted, much will be required.* More or less. He thought it was Matthew, maybe Luke. Didn't matter. Seems there would be a price to be paid.

Fish looked around for Ray but couldn't see him. He poked his head into his trailer. Ray was sound asleep on the couch, curled into a tight circle. Basic boxer. Nothing happening here, go to sleep. "I'm calling it," he said to Aardvark.

"I'm gonna stay out," the A said. "I want to work on something."

Jon had a hunch he should stay out, that whatever the Aard was working out, Jon should know about it. The feeling came and went. Just one feeling, floating like a cloud across a mirror-smooth sky. Here, then gone. He put his hesitation aside and went to bed and slept like a baby, once he got past the snores of his canine friend over on the couch.

He woke early the next morning. It was only a couple of days before the Bend regionals and he realized he was anticipating the action. Tournament weeks were fun, as he had noted before. The week before the tournament especially, because of the camaraderie, the everybody-plays-with-everybody thing. He was now accepted as a good player and could count on getting on the court with anybody on his merits. Not as a horse, a stud, but as a comer, someone who could get the ball back. Somebody who was worth warming up with, at least.

From a 4.0 perspective, he had grown immensely in a very short time and would certainly take some people by surprise. It's said that at the 4.0 level, one knows all the shots and now it's just about consistency. This didn't apply all that much to Fish. He still had plenty of holes in his game, but the constant practice with Aardvark, the continuous discussions they held, Aardvark staying true to form and not saying much but enough and at the right times, never discouraging, never falsely encouraging, just being almost a neutral force, a sounding board for Jon as he worked out what worked and what didn't … all this focus had contributed to making him a more seasoned player in a very short time.

Another thing that helped was Gabby. From time to time Gabby stepped in to play a game or two, and Fish found that if he forcibly took himself out of the 'I'm a guy and better than you' attitude, he enjoyed playing with her immensely and came to treasure her strengths and the time they spent together. It was trippy … even in this tournament week, with her on the court it remained a game and very much part of their courtship, as he had come to think of their relationship. This was the strangest thing; he'd never had many girlfriends who truly interested him, so it was uncharted territory.

It seemed as if they walked protected by destiny, that they were going together to something preordained. He had no thoughts of any other woman other than Gabby. Before this experience women hadn't been a critical factor. He had been more about his career, his sports, his plans. His one dalliance of the year with the nice woman in Palm Creek involved about as much effort as he was willing to put into it.

But this was brand new for him. Gabby was his, and he was hers. The steps they walked through together were making them closer and closer. Even the pickleball divorce, their mini-fight, seemed a distant thing. He could look out and imagine still being with Gabby in ten, twenty, thirty years. Growing old and older together and without being bored. She was the only girl he had ever dated who didn't bore him in some way. There was none of that with her.

Within all these changes came one other. On the pickleball court he realized that he could actually learn from her. She had a very strong athletic background, grew up with badminton and tennis racquets in her hand. Everyone in her family played, including her dad who had coached her with athletics as well as singing. Growing up this way in a family of three older brothers and a dad who could and would kick her butt at any game, she got tough. Her comments to Fish weren't hurtful generally but were very direct as a result. He quickly got to the point where he was counting on her for feedback and this, too, improved his game.

Aardvark, in his usual way, didn't take offense at the possible displacement of some of his coaching role. To the contrary, he obviously liked Gabby, liked having her around almost as much as Fish. Even Ray adopted Gabby into his inner circle, which was unusual as he was not that attracted to human females, bonding more quickly with men. Ray made an exception for her and more than once Fish had looked up from reading to see him on the couch with Gabby, his head in her lap, one hand scratching behind his ears while she tried to hold a book at eye level with the other.

This domestic scene warmed him completely, put him in the moment totally. He never knew that life could slow down like that, and that, sometimes, it would almost stop. A moment would last for a minute, an hour, all night.

Of course, the center could not hold and even this idyllic existence would change. Jon woke up one morning, the morning before the tournament, to find Gabby gone. She had slept over, using the convertible sofa bed while he slept in the bedroom; they went to that without discussing it, still holding each other at arm's length in that way.

But in the morning she was gone. Her mostly restored

and grey-primered Karman Ghia was gone, Jersey was gone. This in itself was unusual, but he didn't think more of it, simply noticed it and went to play pickleball with Aardvark.

Just before the start of the tournament, everyone was ramping up play. He was pretty sure where their competition would come from. Certainly they'd be tested by Pit Bull and Three-Dog. He didn't know how they would play against him and Aardvark as a team, but individually they were very tough. Pit Bull was strong as any ox and Three-Dog was very deceptive, a hard combination.

Pit Bull would come directly at his opponent's upper body from any angle, making control of their returns difficult. To deal with that, Jon and Aard went to an empty court as soon as one vacated and took turns hitting balls at each other as hard as they could. As long as the ball hit clothing there was no pain and no bruising. Fish found this to be great fun, a way to get aggressions out, a harmless way, like having a pillow fight.

Gradually he learned that to take this kind of shot, one had to 'receive' it, not just keep a flat paddle in front of it. The flat paddle would return the ball erratically and often set up a put-away by the opponents. Instead, Aard showed him that taking the ball with a tiny paddle motion back toward the body softened receipt of the shot, allowing him to drop the ball back softly. The objective was to both soften and direct the ball and by mid-day they were both doing better. Not perfect, but better.

"Have you seen Gabby?" Fish said eventually. "I thought she would be here."

Aard looked at him oddly. "I saw her this morning. She was leaving with Jersey."

The news felt strange to him, like a soft punch in his gut.

*Why would she leave now? Without telling him?* "Did she say anything else?"

"She didn't need to." He shrugged. "I told her to go."

Fish felt his face flush. It was the beginning of a rage he had only experienced a couple of times in his life. The violation of a trust; his friend, perhaps his only real friend, was getting between him and perhaps the only love he had had.

"Why did you do that?" Fish felt his voice quivering and knew his decibel level was a bit high.

"There's something I needed her to do. Something that involves the two of you." Aardvark looked at Jon straight on, very calm. "Something I can't tell you about yet." After a second he added, "You have to trust me on this."

There had been only a few times in Jon's entire life when he simply didn't know what to do. He didn't even know what to say to Aardvark. He had agreed early on to take Aardvark into his life at a very deep level as his life coach, his mentor. But that didn't include Aardvark making decisions for him. This felt exactly like that, that he should have been involved.

"You're an asshole." His voice was very tight, almost ready to break.

"Maybe," said Aardvark. "She said the same thing."

Jon didn't trust himself to speak, so he walked away. He tried to shake off the news but couldn't. He had just admitted to himself that he and Gabby were — or perhaps at least he was falling in love — and now she was gone, for the moment anyway. He felt a great longing for her, as if he absolutely had to have her, but for some reason Aardvark knew and he didn't, that that wasn't appropriate at this moment.

He called her. Her cell dumped directly into voicemail,

signaling that her phone was off. Her message was her norm, the Joe Walsh line, 'Leave me a message. Maybe I'll call.'

He walked back to Aardvark, who was taping a bit of lead to the top of his paddle. "You got anything more you can say?"

It was Aardvark's turn to be silent for a moment. "I wouldn't have asked Gabby to do this if it was possible to accomplish the objective in a different way," he said at last.

The afternoon became a bit surreal. Much of the gain he had made as a player over these months began to dissipate, to disappear like a summer fog. He began to overcompensate without knowing it. Drop shots went very high and were slammed, corrections threw the same shot into the net again, as if he hadn't practiced at all. His serve, rock-solid front and backhand, started to waver and the number of serves he got in dropped from maybe ninety-five percent or more to maybe eighty percent or less on the backhand and less than that on the forehand. Plus his serve was shorter; as his muscles contracted, he lost his sense of the back line. His confidence eroded almost before his eyes.

Aardvark, who noticed everything, of course noticed this. "Can I help?" he asked at one point — the most frontal acknowledgement of Jon's struggles that he had ever made.

"I don't know what you'd do," Jon said. "You've already done too much."

"I could tell you to put Gabby aside, for the moment."

"You could tell me more about why you sent her away. But you won't."

"I don't think I can. But you could view it as part of your

Practice."

"Is that an order?" Jon felt himself getting testy. "I don't like you making decisions for me. I don't like anybody doing that."

"I'm not. In fact, I can't do that," said Aard. "Ultimately, it'll just turn out to be a suggestion. I know you're pissed. But you might as well make use of the bad times, too."

Jon thought about that again during the early evening. He and Ray had finished a small run a few times around the campground and he was drinking water, trying to increase his hydration. He remembered reading something in a book about meditation. The writer frequently suggested what Aard had just said. Use the strong emotions, even the very negative ones, as the focus item for meditation sessions. Once you can let go of the strong negative emotions, not being attached to or focused on them, you can more easily deal with the ups and downs of life. Something like that.

He took his chair over to the edge of the pond, started the stopwatch function for future reference, and began to follow his breath down into his emotions. He pictured Gabby's face before him. As the breath deepened and slowed, he kept coming back to her image in his mind. Like any thought the image would not stay still. It came and went.

Eventually, however, he was able to establish something of a rhythm — her image and his breath came and went. When he inhaled, her image came up from the bottom of his mental 'screen' like swiping upward on an iPhone. He allowed it to dissolve into pixels in his mind.

At the end of the session Jon spent a minute or two re-orientating to the reality he had left. More and more he found that his meditation sessions were becoming a different form of reality and one that for the most part he preferred. He knew that some Buddhist monks who were very ill had actually died during meditation, moving on to the next step in the most peaceful way imaginable. Death was a terrifying thing to him, the ultimate unknown, the most profound loss of control. He could imagine dying would be like meditation, just scarier.

He looked at his watch and was shocked to find that he had spent almost two hours in this single meditation session, double his normal long session. This was way longer than any meditation session he had done before. And it felt like a moment. At the same time, he realized that there he was again, measuring meditation sessions on his personal suck-o-meter. Attachment. Grasping. But in the peace of the after-session he also realized that didn't matter, not at all.

After a few minutes Aardvark came up with his own chair. "Can I sit here?" he asked.

"Yeah. You can." Jon paused. "I'm gonna trust you on the Gabby thing," he said after awhile.

"Cool," Aardvark said. "Sorry I had to do it this way …"

*Hmm,* Jon said to himself. *Jury's out …*

They faced outward to the pond. It was twilight and a few small bats were working the mosquitoes and mayflies on the lake. "I caught a bat on a fly one time," Aardvark said.

"I did, too," said Jon. "California Mosquito, #18," he added. "Barbless."

"Release him?" the Aard asked, idly.

"Nope. Pan-fried him and ate him. Tasted like chicken."

The Aardvark gave him a look and clucked his tongue.

Jon looked back calmly. "What?" he asked.

After a few seconds of silence, Aardvark added a thought. "Good to see you're feeling better."

Jon couldn't argue with that and didn't. Anyway, Jon had actually caught a bat on two occasions and once had hooked and landed a big dragonfly on the same fly, a tiny California Mosquito.

Ray had become used to moving around the lake in his search for the perfect frog each evening and Jon was allowing him to run pretty much free, without a leash. This wasn't allowed, of course, and when Jon saw the headlights of an approaching golf cart he suspected the topic of conversation.

"Fish," said the camp host, a grey-haired work camper named Eddie, "you gotta keep this guy on lead!" Ray, who was sitting next to Eddie on the golf cart's front seat, looked up at him fondly, leaned over and licked his arm. "I'm getting complaints!"

"No, you're not," said Fish. "Tell the truth." He gestured toward Ray like Raphael had during his speech when he got all the dogs to sit with him. Ray didn't move.

"Well, my boss would complain, if she was here," Eddie said.

"Lydia lives in Florence. That's hours from here," Aardvark added. He gestured at Ray and Ray hopped out of the cart and went and sat next to him.

Eddie grinned and left. Fish went over and clipped a lead on Ray just to be law-abiding. He looked at Aardvark. "Did you teach Raphael that move? The one you just did?"

"Maybe," said Aardvark.

"Tell me. Did you teach it to Raphael?"

"If I say 'yes' then you will say I have to teach you," Aardvark grinned good-naturedly. "So, no."

"I'm going to bed. Tomorrow will be a big day," Jon said,

giving up for the moment.

"It'll be another day," Aardvark agreed. "They're all big."

~

Tournament days are very long and Jon had already found it doesn't pay to get to them too early; on the other hand, he felt antsy just lying in bed. Too much time on his hands, what with Gabby gone and a 10 a.m. start for his bracket. He got up, called Gabby, got no answer again, and took Ray out to run a few miles. Nothing big, just cruising. The dog, he noted, was in amazing shape, especially for a boxer with no decent breathing apparatus inside that pushed in clown-face. He wasn't even slobbering much at the end of the run.

By extension, he realized he was physically in the best shape of his life. His recent weight was down to 195 pounds, very low for him. He even felt lean so his body fat was most like equally low. His respiratory functions were terrific and he attributed part of that improvement to meditation. Staying with his own breath each morning was increasing his lung capacity, he was sure of it. The occasional dizzy spells he suffered from, which he had long attributed to poor hydration, were seemingly a thing of the past. He felt pretty darn ready to play … physically.

Mentally, not so much. A part of him was with Gabby. He didn't know what was going on. He didn't attach to it as much, having worked through most of that with the meditation. But he flat missed her. There was no denying it. This was the first time he had had this level of attachment, way beyond anything even in his short marriage. He was fifty-two, soon fifty-three. True love had come late in life for him. He had never thought he'd be in this position.

He looked over his tournament gear and decided to wear his grey outfit with the vaguely Zen-like red inscriptions on front and back of the shirt. Holding up the shirt staring at it, he decided to ask Aardvark if he knew what it said. After the tournament, though. He didn't need any more to think about.

With shoes, of course, he broke out the rainbow-colored Lozan Liis. These were his only tournament shoes, and something about them made his feet very happy. When asked, he told people it was about the way they breathed. That was, he knew, essentially crap. It was the way they looked. Tying them on he remembered Aardvark's comments on them the first time they met, way back in Palm Creek. He stretched a bit, doing Achilles stretches against the door, and when he was through he walked out to roust Aardvark.

"I see you, Jon," called Aardvark from across the way.

"And I see you, Aardvark," he said in response. A very comforting ritual, in spite of the recent stress between them. Rituals were important. Connections were important. Family and friends were important. He had learned a few things in the last few months.

Driving in together in his Kia, they talked a bit, mostly about strategy. The draws for the brackets had been posted the night before and they were in pretty good shape. Jon didn't want a bye, a free first-round pass; he'd much prefer a good warm-up, and he had been worried that their recent little win at Thousand Trails would have pushed them too far up in the seeding. But they had gotten away with it and had what he considered a pretty easy match, a team of brothers, Tom and Perry Sanders. Tom was actually rated as a 3.5 and Jon thought he was just playing with Perry for the fun of it. Odds are they wouldn't be too difficult, unless Aardvark decided as the de facto court manager that they had to do something weird like both playing off-handed.

From there the rest of the bracket looked tough. To him it looked unlikely that they would meet Pit Bull and

A. J. Fraties

Three-Dog anywhere early, but he knew if they kept moving through the four of them would hook up down the line. Then there was the Captain and Noel the Mole, a long-time team and very strong together.

"I think that we're gonna be at this a while," Jon said. "I'd like to get a good warm-up out of this first match."

"Let's not take too much for granted," Aardvark said. "But I agree with you. Let's see if we can get a good lead early. If we do, we can use a bit more practice. But ..."

"Yeah, I know ... if you assume something ... " Jon said. They simultaneously said the next line, "It makes an ass out of you and me!" They smiled at each other and at one of the world's oldest but most-true clichés.

The Bend tournament itself was always well organized. Better than that was the wonderful venue. The pickleball complex in Pine Nursery Park was a spectacular setting, stately trees lining one side, grass mounts with picnic tables and rugged mountains in the west usually covered with snow. A natural-scape dog park sits to the east, and for good measure a nice fishing pond is just south, giving the athletes somewhere different to stretch between matches.

Anne had vendors strung out across the west side as well, with multi-colored food trucks interspersed everywhere there was a space. This, Fish thought, was the only tournament that cared about the colors of the food trucks. Pretty nice.

Part of the excitement of any pickleball event in Bend is because of the cast of characters. And the timing for the tournament was critical as well. Late summer in Bend means good outdoor weather. When they arrived, Fish could see TV crews already filming, drones overhead capturing birds-eye views of the courts, and a dozen neighborhood kids with fishing poles, soccer balls, or skateboards watching the pros play on the west courts. Pit Bull was watching the pros as well and Fish walked back to chat with him.

"How you guys feeling?" he asked the Bull. "Lousy, I hope?"

"Oh, man. It's my hip. I shouldn't even be playing," PB whined, stretching a bit. "I'm thinking we should just forfeit and save the grief."

"Shoot. Sorry to hear that," Jon said. "Should we go find Anne and get you taken off now?"

Pit Bull nodded distractedly. "Well, let's wait and see," he said. "Maybe I can walk it off."

Jon smiled to himself as he walked away. Nobody in the world was less likely to forfeit a match than the Bull. He'd play if his hip was missing. And speaking of missing ... he called Gabby again. And again, no answer. He had thought maybe ... it didn't matter. Focus on the now, he told himself. *We've got matches to play.*

This was appropriate self-talk. When he and Aardvark got on the court for their first match they quickly realized that the two brothers were more than okay. The fact that Tom was rated lower, as a 3.5, didn't mean squat given that they had obviously played together a bunch. They were an intuitive pair, each covering well for the other with very good movement.

In spite of their good movement, however, they were overmatched against Aardvark and Fish. That was soon obvious. Fish and Aard got off to a slow start and dropped back a couple of points on unforced errors on a pair of Aardvark's missed hero shots, but won the last eight points to finish the first game 11-5.

They could see one glaring hole, which was primarily on Tom's backhand. It was a simple thing. He didn't go far enough toward the ball when he was setting up on a backhand. He stopped about a foot short of where he should stop. This made him erratic. Being a bit erratic, generally stretching too much, Tom would put the ball up. With his strength and quickness, Aardvark could put all of those away and anything he couldn't get to, Fish could easily cover with his reach. With this in mind, they could just focus on Tom's backhand and make the second game a piece of cake. Except, of course, for Aardvark.

Between games they were changing sides and Aardvark came over to Fish. "What say we tell Tom what we saw in that game?"

"You mean tell him he's stretching on his backhand?"

"Exactly. It would make the game better. We talked about that," Aardvark said.

"We talked about getting a good workout," Jon said. "Not about giving unsolicited advice."

"Well, this would help us get a better warm-up," Aard said. "Anyway," he grinned wolfishly, "if we get in trouble we've got a shot that they would never get back."

"Really?" said Fish, interested. "Which one?"

"Enrique lob," said Aardvark. This time it was Fish's turn to grin. The Enrique Lob, named for the pro who does it best, isn't an easy shot to hit by any means. It's hit from the kitchen line, seven feet from the net. The person executing the shot has to be able to reach a dink, or soft shot, in the air. Taking it in the air as a volley, the executor flips the ball over the weak shoulder side of the opponent. By the time the opponent realizes the shot has been hit, the ball is past them and they have to scramble like mad to even get a paddle on it.

"'K," Jon said. "I'm in."

The referee was hanging over the top of the net between

courts chatting with his counterpart who was conducting warmups for a match next door and hadn't called them back to the line. Aardvark called Tom and Eddie over.

"You guys are playing well," he said. "But can I mention something that maybe help you? Please say 'no' if you don't want to hear it, really!"

Nobody would say 'no' to that question. "Sure," said Tom. Eddie nodded. "Tom, you are playing great. But when you cover those backhand dinks, you're stopping a half foot or so from the ball. As a result, you're stretching a little and you wind up having to flick the ball over off your wrist. Maybe consider getting a little closer and you won't pop the ball up off the stretch. Like I said, it just might take 'good' to 'great.'"

Tom and Eddie looked at each other. "I *do* do that, don't I?" Tom said ruefully.

"I guess so," said his brother. "Ball's been a little high sometimes."

It's always interesting to see a good coach work with another person. Jon observed how straightforward Aardvark's critique was. Few would have taken offense at the way the criticism was offered, and Tom hadn't. Rare skill, he thought.

Time in was called and game two began. Each time they dinked to Tom's backhand, they saw him consciously moving more. And his results improved, especially when he got right in front of the ball. He seemed much more comfortable with hitting the dink and several times surprised Aardvark and Fish with excellent placement of a shot that previously was just a moon-ball set-up for an easy put away.

This, however, didn't cause the game to be remarkably better. Rallies did last a little longer, Fish thought. So they were getting what they wanted out of the deal, a better warm-up. They won the game 11-7, never being threatened, really. On the last point of the game Aardvark hit one perfect Enrique Lob ... otherwise they kept that one in reserve.

After the game Fish and Aardvark hung around on the court for an extra minute. "I thought that went well," said Aardvark.

"You're a great coach," said Fish, meaning it. "That was exactly what Tom needed and when he needed it."

"Remember that," said Aardvark. "That last part."

"What and when?"

"Un-huh." Aardvark wiped off his paddle with a yellow microfiber towel he had brought onto the court. "When Gabby gets back."

"Do you ever stop being so friggin' mysterious?" said Fish, irritated.

"An enigma wrapped in a conundrum," the Aardvark whispered to add mystery. "I've always wanted to use that in a conversation."

The bracket, full at thirty-two teams, was moving along well and they rapidly got their next match, remarkably, a cakewalk. They played against two folks they knew well but who had hardly ever scored more than five points against them. Since everybody had their tournament faces on, Fish had expected this match to be tougher. But actually, it was no exception. It was the quickest two-game match Fish remembered winning in his few tournaments.

The only hitch was his forehand serve, which for a moment gave him a start, flying out long both times he made an error. This could have preceded his actually losing his serve again, but both times he went to his backhand on the next opportunity and got both of those balls in.

"Nice having the backhand serve, isn't it?" said Aardvark, too casually.

"Is that an 'I told you so'?" Fish asked.

"Well, didn't I?"

Fish knew that the Aard had, in fact, given him that instruction and he certainly remembered using the serve 100 percent of the time at Thousand Trails. *Yes, you did*, he said, but only to himself.

The next match, their third, was a bit more challenging, taking them three games to win. The difficulty, again, was his serve. *It's the wind*, he initially thought. Wind is a usual thing at Pine Nursery Park and when it was behind him he began to throw more shots long. When they switched sides in the second game he quickly realized the reverse was true — into the wind, with him stiffening a bit with anxiety, his forehand was a bit strained and his shots were short. Still, since he had talked and journaled about serves and wind endlessly, he saw the pattern. He finally stopped fighting the wind and settled down and in a very workmanlike fashion they won the last two games and the match.

With several matches now behind them, they were deep in the heart of the bracket. It looked to Fish that this could be the place they would meet Pit Bull and Three-Dog, who were waiting in chairs watching the match, scoping their next opponents.

With a wait of an hour or so before he and Aard were up again, he wanted to keep himself warm during that period.

"I'm gonna go over and walk around the pond for a while," he said to Aardvark.

"Sounds good. I'll come and get you if anything speeds up."

Fish and Ray strolled the short distance to the pond and Fish removed his friend's leash. "Behave," he said.

Ray wagged his short tail and walked over to the shallow pond's edge. A number of fish were cruising by, singles and pairs. The trim dog sat, cocked his head like the RCA Victor mascot, and watched the fish. He was remarkably focused for a boxer, Fish believed. Not a breed that tolerates boredom, he thought. Something to be learned there.

He had walked the perimeter and was beginning the second lap when the big grey heron who had been fishing flapped up into flight. Following the bird's flight he caught sight of Gabby, her little mutt Jersey sitting nearby. She was standing by a small willow tree, dressed in a summer green pickleball outfit, her red hair gleaming. Her long, slim fingers were clasped in front of her below her waist. She was beautiful and his heart tripped over itself.

"I see you, Gabby," he said.

"I see you, Jon," she replied. "I love you."

Neither she nor Fish had said that to the other. It had seemed way too soon, like sleeping together. Not at all necessary to be said, until she said it. Then it seemed to Fish that that was the best thing she could have said. He suddenly felt very whole, better than he could remember feeling. Maybe ever.

"I love you, too, Gabby," he said, the words feeling natural. Without taking his eyes from her, Jon walked toward her. Ray spotted her just as he said the magic words and ran, reaching her before Jon did, giving her little dog a friendly head butt and then putting his muddy paws up on her midriff.

"You are a pig," Gabby reproved the dog in a mock-serious tone. She took his paws off her and dropped him back to the ground. Ray wagged furiously, obviously not caring about the reproof at all. Fish wondered what kind of a hold she had on Ray. Somehow, she hadn't even gotten dirty with the boxer's pond mud. Fish wondered absently how she could do that, too. Clearly, he had not read the last page with this woman, and this was a book he thought he'd have tons of fun reading. He suddenly felt ... what? ... *glad*, he thought.

Aardvark came up behind her. "Hi, Gabby," he said. "About time to roll, Fish."

"PB and Three-Dog won," Jon stated, no question.

"Nope," said the Aard. "They lost. To the Captain and the Mole. PB was bitching about his hip."

"Wow." Fish was shocked. "He had said something earlier but I thought it was just his usual BS. What's he gonna do?"

"No worries," said Aardvark. "I fixed him. His hip was almost out of its socket."

"How'd you do that?"

Aardvark looked at him and smiled.

"Got it," said Fish. "Powers." Gabby grinned and Aardvark nodded. Approvingly, Fish thought.

"I didn't think it was fair to fix him during the medical time-out they took," Aardvark said. "Get what you earn, right?"

"Yeah, I guess," Fish said. "You could have waited until after we play 'em." He was pretty sure PB, injured or well, would find a way to win the consolation bracket and he and Three-Dog would be back to see them in the gold-silver finals.

"I'm sure you want their very best game when we play them, right?"

"No," said Fish. "When it comes to PB, I'd rather have his very worst game."

"You don't mean that." Gabby pretended shock.

"Yes, I do," said Fish. "Those two both have tons of game, sick or well. I could handle an easy win!"

Gabby and Fish walked back to the courts holding hands very naturally. Fish liked it. He felt like he was part of something. A family. Ray and Jersey trotted ahead, trailing their leads, keeping exact pace with the Aardvark. *All my family except the 'rents*, he thought.

"We have a lot to talk about," Gabby said.

"Yes, we do," agreed Fish. "But not now."

"Later. Not now," she nodded. She squeezed his hand. All will be well.

As Aardvark had said, the feeder match in front of them ended and the four contestants were still on the court, chatting. Jon and Aardvark would play the winners, the Captain and Noel the Mole. Fish nodded to the Captain, a long, lanky former marine with a near-bald head excepting the tufts of hair brushed artlessly back around his ears. The Captain was always tough, uniformly good-natured, and had a game that matched up to Fish's, both left-handed, both tall, both looking for shots they could put away. You can't teach aggressiveness, and they were both aggressive players. Fish had won some, lost some against the Captain.

Fish also nodded to Marie, the Captain's wife, standing outside the gate. Marie was short, trim, blonde and good-looking. One way of getting into the Captain's head was to hit on his wife, so Fish winked at her. She raised her eyebrows and grinned. The Captain noticed the interchange and wagged a long finger at Fish, then dragged his finger across his throat, his meaning unmistakable. Fish gave a big 'Who, me?' shrug and then a thumbs-up on the good win. The Captain touched the brim of his Semper Fi baseball hat and took a little bow. Competitors sometimes, friends always.

"Maybe we have even more to talk about than I thought!" said Gabby, waving at Marie.

The Captain's partner, as usual, was Noel the Mole, a short, muscular guy with a scruffy blondish-red beard and pronounced calf muscles from years of lifting. The Mole probably got his nickname because not many things rhymed with 'Noel.' Fish thought the Mole was probably the most underrated player in the top tier of the 4.0s. His game was far from flashy. The proof is how you play and he could keep up, especially on the short game. You could dink with him for a while, but you couldn't out-dink him. He had great patience.

The other remarkable thing about the Mole's game was his ability to hit overheads. Because he was maybe 5' 7", a trifle shorter than average, people naturally tried to lob him. But he had a marvelous musculature that allowed him to get back of those lobs, curve his back and power forward off that curve, tweaking off those huge calves like a snap off a martial arts reverse punch. Lots of power from little movement, a tightly coiled spring. If the Mole had any weakness, and Fish wasn't sure he did, it was extending rallies too long, not ending them when he could. But Fish had learned more about this subject and no longer considered long rallies that bad a thing.

Fish knew he and Aardvark could be in trouble against these two. Adding to the problem was that the Captain and the Mole had never beaten Pit Bull and Three-Dog before and were sure to be riding on a cloud as they went into their next match against Fish and Aardvark. Even if they lost against Fish and Aard, they would only drop down to the consolation bracket where they'd immediately be playing for at least a bronze medal if they lost again there.

That little bit of complacency could work against the Captain and the Mole, feeling secure, losing that edge. On the other hand, Jon knew that taking them for granted would just create his own complacency and could get him and the Aard in big trouble quickly.

All these thoughts rattling around! Fish knew he had a tendency to over analyze things, proved out once again when he walked over to check in with Aardvark. "How do you feel about playing these guys?" he asked casually.

"Good!" said Aardvark. "Nice guys. Play well. We can learn something. What more could you want?"

"What I could want is an easy path to the gold-silver match," Fish said. Ray looked up at the tone in his master's voice. Fish ruffled the dog's neck.

"Have you ever heard of The Law of Parsimony?"

Fish thought. "Seems I haven't. Am I going to be sorry?"

Aardvark had a great toothy smile when he was greatly amused. "Yes, you are," he said.

Right now, looking at Aardvark, Fish believed he had never seen so many teeth, except in pictures of a saltwater crocodile, and those, he remembered, could weigh over 2,000 pounds. Otherwise, strong family resemblance, he thought.

## Chapter Thirty-Two

"THE LAW OF PARSIMONY," Aardvark continued, "is more often known as Occam's Razor."

"Right, right," Fish said, snapping his fingers. "Shortest distance between two points is a straight line."

"Yep. Also, the simplest solution is usually the right one."

"Why does this discussion make me nervous?" Fish tapped his paddle handle against the fence-rail.

"Probably for good reason, grasshoppah," said the Aard.

What followed was a very detailed conversation about where Fish was in relation to his goals. In the Aardvark's view, Fish had long ago achieved one level of pickleball mastery by working through some of the various issues around his serve. But the final test of that would be to create the most stressful situation they possibly could and make him — in essence — serve his way out of trouble. To overcome, once and for all, the symptom that plagued him.

"... and still bothers you, if you admit it," said the A.

"This is ridiculous," said Fish. "I don't even know what a situation like that would look like! Plus, I don't think it would prove anything we haven't already done together."

"If you got through this test, it would be the last major hurdle." The Aardvark was a bit distracted with a knotted shoelace but looked up to see his reaction.

"You've been reading too much *Hero's Journey* again," scoffed Fish, recalling the trials and tests in the famous work on hero development.

"See," said the Aardvark. "See how much of a fun guy you can be? Basically, the how is easy. You have to serve everything forehand. You would no longer have the failsafe of your backhand serve just in case. You've got to make it on the forehand alone."

Jon got it. He flashed on that tournament, way back at the beginning of the journey when he and Kirk were only a couple of points away from a victory and his fears had taken over.

Fish felt an odd tightening in his gut. He recognized it immediately; it was the feeling he got whenever he was moving toward losing the serve. He looked around, trying to distract himself. "Why should I do it?"

"To move through," said Aardvark. "To become the player and the person you can be. To Arrive."

Arrive. The word resonated with Fish. It was clear that relative to the A's family, Fish at least had made it to the finish line. But now he needed to cross the line. He needed to take on the biggest challenge of all, the wrestling match in his own mind.

All this flashed in seconds, but it was now very straightforward and why Aardvark had called it an Occam's Razor solution. In the detective books the police always look at the butler or the husband or wife as the murderer because, most often, they are. It's efficient to do this. It's the straightest line to the solution using the least resources.

Likewise, here. He had all the tools he needed even without his backup serve. But he now knew the serve was just the manifestation of other stuff in his head. It was the manifestation of him, his inner self. He wasn't enough of a psychologist to know if it was some appearance of shame, the expectations he carried inside himself from an earlier age, or what. It was here, though. And if he didn't work through it now it would simply appear again as something other than his serve, and again it would be something that he would have to deal with, and again he'd be working on the symptoms, which were distractions, and not with the problem, which was him.

"Damn," he said.

"I take that as a 'yes'?" confirmed the Aardvark, looking off into the distance.

"Damn!" repeated Jon, a bit more emphatically.

"A definite 'yes'," Aardvark nodded.

Fish had spent too much time over-analyzing this subject. He knew that many people go through their pickleball careers and never lose their serve at all. To them it seems impossible to lose a serve, and they'll literally say that. But once you do lose your serve, it's like the 'yips' in golf. The feeling is in you like a virus, always waiting somewhere just above your stomach. The feeling is hard to explain.

Its onset, however, is easy to know and to explain. For Jon, it was like a panic attack. He could feel his body and mind going somewhere very, very uncomfortable. In the past he couldn't stop it, and that lack of control was frightening. Some have defined neurotic anxiety clinically as a "free-floating fear," meaning it doesn't have a target. You're not afraid of not paying the rent, you are afraid that some awful, unnamed thing will happen. This is a certain knowledge. The question isn't whether or not that thing will happen, or when the slavering beast will appear at the doorway to your cave. It will. You just don't know the exact nature of it, when it will happen or even where, and those unknowns make the whole thing worse.

So, losing one's serve is essentially pickleball's equivalent of a panic attack. A long, sustained panic attack accompanied by great feelings of shame and loss of worth. After all, in pickleball, if you can't serve, what good are you? All your friends, associates, and competitors, not to mention family and the church pastor, will be there for the occasion. They will all offer advice. None of it will work. If you had a towel, you could throw it in, because you are through for the day.

Worse, a pickleball panic attack typically lasted beyond the day. Jon might get out a few days later and try to put it out of his mind as a one-off event, but he knew that if he let it get into his mind, even now, it would be there for at least the next couple of matches. So his agreeing to this was under duress, and all because he wanted two other things more than winning the match.

First, Fish realized, that, yes, he wanted to put this serving thing to bed, and without the crutch of another serve; in his case, his backhand serve. He was surprised to find that he did want that, especially since he had not reacted well to it even a few moments ago when Aardvark had brought it up. But he did. It was like getting off meds. The backhand serve had been his safety net, but maybe it was time to go cold turkey.

And, second, he wanted to Arrive. Early in his journey he didn't have thought of arriving anywhere because nobody had told him there was anywhere to Arrive. Mostly the journey itself was touted as the big benefit. Even his mother, bless her perceptive little heart, had said that much. "Jon, don't try to overthink things out there. It's your exploration that's the value, not where you go."

Now he saw things differently. The journey itself would always be of value, true enough. But he thought now that was only for people who didn't know there really was somewhere to go. If you weren't aware there could be a destination, the only thing you had left to value was the journey. And of course, the only way to Arrive, per

Aardvark, was Through.

And he knew now that even the Arrival was only the beginning. What lay beyond that? What else would he be expected to learn or know or experience or somehow deal with? What talents would he be given? What responsibilities did he have to those talents? Or to himself, for that matter? There were far more questions than answers.

When stuck on meaning-of-life questions, do something practical. He went and found his pickleball bag and began overwrapping the handles of the paddles he thought he would use. Then he took out a new rawhide bone and tossed it to Ray, who promptly made a circle next to Jersey and lay down to keep his back between the other dog and the bone. Fish rooted around, found a smaller bone and held it up so Gabby could see it. She nodded permission and he tossed it to the smaller dog who put it between his paws and started working it. They were in the shade of the trees here, a cool enough place, and the dogs could busy themselves gnawing while the match took place.

Fish grabbed his water bottle and his two paddles and went toward the court. Gabby intercepted him, squeezed his shoulders with her strong hands. "Play with today's game," she said, and hugged him.

*Good advice,* he thought. Today he'd have a different game by design. Not so much wondering about 'who shows up,' more like … well … let me take one of the long irons out of the bag and play with a smaller number of clubs. Or whatever the pickleball equivalent of that would be.

Fish and the Aardvark hadn't played for a while. The referee wasn't on the court yet so they took advantage of that. Fish's serves were good thus far. Deep in the depths he could feel monsters lurking, but for now they were sidelined. He boomed forehand after forehand into the backcourt to Aardvark, who moved around the serving box to give him different angles to shoot at. For the most part, he would be trying to keep everything deep and to the backhand and would try to remember he had a fellow lefty across from him.

Aardvark, in turn, was returning balls in interesting ways. He would go in and short-hop the first, go back very deep behind the baseline and take the next on the drop at the last possible moment. He was also experimenting with returns, usually placing them mid-court and mid-deep but from all the different angles he was giving Fish.

After the warm-up and as the match was being called to play, Aardvark walked out with Jon where they would receive serve. "You're pretty amped-up," the A said.

"True enough. Any suggestions?"

"Under hit the first return," said Aardvark. Jon knew exactly what he was saying. His adrenaline would make up for any lack of normal distance.

"Also, your warm-up tells me you'll be playing very well today. But this has to be a challenge. So I might have to add something."

"Like what?" said Fish, nearing his ready position.

"Let's wait and see," called over Aard. "Stay tuned!"

The Captain and the Mole were a stacking team, but Jon and Aard had decided not to stack against them. Stacking is done to enable teams to keep strong hands in the middle and not rotate them out of that position as would normally be the case for the serving team when they score points. There are pluses and minuses to stacking, but Jon and Aard had discussed this and thought they'd just play them straight up.

They were playing with new DuraMax 40 balls, a very bright-yellow ball, which probably could be seen from the moon. But right from the beginning, Jon felt the ball was moving very slowly, rotating so slowly that he could have easily counted all the holes. He stepped into the Captain's side-spinning serve and under-hit the return with a bit of top-spin. To his amazement the ball went all the way to the back line.

"Told you," said Aard. They won that exchange on Captain's wide return. Jon took the ball, tossed it, and hit it as naturally as could be. His forehand serve curved left to right into the Captain's body, and the Captain, playing way too close to the baseline, couldn't quite handle it. It was just one point, but it was game on and the white hats were winning.

Later Gabby asked and Jon really didn't remember anything about the first half of this match. He had had no conscious concern about his forehand serve, no worries about anything. He was in each point completely. If he had had a phrase to describe himself it would have been 'completely competent.' He was a perfect team player, backing up Aard when he needed it, staying out of his way when he didn't need him, and generally being, he thought, unexciting.

This was not, however, what the crowd saw. The Men's 4.0 division is one of the most popular. But because of the players, you could have set any other 4.0 match on fire that day and it wouldn't have attracted as much interest as this one. It was clear to everyone who had been watching previous matches that there were six really good players in the 4.0s today. And four of those players were still in the winners' bracket and were going to give the crowd a show.

After a while, Jon looked over at Gabby in the grandstands just to make contact. She was sitting next to Marie and the two of them saw his glance and as one tossed their heads to their right. Following, he saw that the local TV station, KJNZ 21, had set up and was filming them. This was a big deal for someone like him who had always wanted waves of adulation breaking at his feet. But for some reason, today this made little difference to him.

Jon still wasn't paying any attention to the score and was amazed when he heard he was serving at 10-6 possible game point. He floated through his delivery and hit a beautiful, deep, heavy serve. The Mole handled it but made a tactical error by short-hopping it. Mole's return of serve floated back, just clearing the net and after bouncing in the kitchen kicked up into the easiest put-away opportunity Jon had seen. Careful to take the kitchen line into account, using his long body for leverage, he snapped the ball cross-court and off the court. A no-return game winner. Jon, modest, turned to the back of the line but was delighted. For a moment.

"Foot-fault," called the Aardvark, pointing at Jon. Everyone in the gallery was shocked, the referee was shocked, the Captain and the Mole were nonplused. The ball had already come past the kitchen line when Jon hit it, and there was no way that Jon had been even close enough to the line to touch it. And yet, there was that call.

"C'mon," said Jon, his voice going up an octave. "No way I foot-faulted!" He turned to the referee. "Ref, did you see it?"

"Yeah, I was watching," said the referee, Gin. "No fault!"

"My call, and I saw a foot-fault, sad to say." Aardvark wasn't going to engage in a conversation about it, obviously. "Isn't it side-out?"

Gin called the four opponents together. "This is my call if I saw it," he said, looking straight at the Aard. "And I saw it. No fault. Your point," he said to Fish. "And your game!"

The Aardvark remained very cool. "I believe that's an

incorrect call. May we have a tournament director?"

The Mole looked across the net. "C'mon, Aardvark, let's do this!" The Captain put a hand on the Aardvark's shoulder. "I agree, soldier. You won. Let's move!"

It was Aardvark's right to press the point, even though he didn't have a chance to win it. Rules aren't made for exceptions like this, but responsibilities are clear enough. If a referee sees a foot fault he calls it, and if he sees there is no foot fault, by extension, that is his call. Nonetheless Aardvark could, and did, ask for a tournament director. Thomas, the Assistant Tournament Director, and Anne both came over and verified the decision and the game was finally and officially, over.

Jon had been pissed at the Aardvark a few times recently for setting up weird situations; serving only backhand or forehand or calling foot faults for practice as examples. But here was a case where they hadn't agreed to anything at all. "What the hell was that all about? You know there was no foot fault."

Aardvark eyed him. "Correct, grasshoppah. No foot fault."

"Well, if nothing else, that's rude as hell. You wasted everybody's time on a nonsense call, and for no good reason!" He could feel himself getting stoked up. He wanted to hit something, maybe break a paddle. The heat ran up the back of his neck.

"It's for your good," Aardvark said.

"Well, if your object is to have me play like shit, you've probably succeeded!'

"We don't want you playing like shit. But you have to be out of the zone."

Now Fish got it. Going in, his worry was his serve. But he came in on a roll and dropped into a place where everything was half-speed. He was, in fact, in the zone and didn't want to leave it. Who would? There was no sense of anxiety around his serve in the state he was in ... or at least, the state he had been in. No way he'd be there now.

He reached his paddle over. He and Aardvark touched tips. This had all been about him. How could he resent that? "Just don't do anything else, 'K?" he asked.

"Only if I need to," his friend said, enigmatically.

The time-out and change of side over, Jon began serving. He was now thinking about his serve. That's the first step to meltdown, he thought. But he got that serve in anyway.

# Chapter Thirty-Three

IN SPITE OF Jon's and Aardvark's dominance in the first game, the two teams were evenly matched. Most outsiders would have given the odds to the Aardvark and Fish on firepower alone, but Jon knew better.

Unfortunately, Aardvark hit two uncharacteristic shots into the top of the net early on in the second game. Even with the Aard's skills, Jon didn't imagine the guy could do that on purpose. But they started a couple of points down and traded punches back and forth. Pickleball is a game of short runs, where commonly one team might score two or three points before giving up the side; not so in this game. Everything was literally one point at a time, a grind, all four grinding it out.

Good pickleball players have both hard and soft games. As one example of the soft game, there is a shot sequence called cross-court dinking in which the opposing players at the kitchen line hit diagonal shots to their opponents' sideline. These diagonal shots can continue indefinitely with skilled players, and both the Aardvark and the Mole could do this until the cows came home and today they did. Twenty, thirty shot rallies became the norm between them, with Fish and the Captain simply looking for a mis-hit ball they could poach if it traveled high as it passed their body. Most good cross-court dinks are hit fairly close to the net, though, and Jon and the Captain seldom had a real chance to get in there. Most exchanges were won on the opponent's unforced error, most commonly the Aard or the Mole hitting into the net or hitting the ball wide and out of bounds. If Jon or the Captain did get into the play, one of them would often break the action, rip a ball or two, and then, like as not, they'd all return to the same cross-court pattern.

Patience was the key; waiting for the right opportunity was crucial. One lapse of focus would result in a point or a side-out. Even with all the classy cross-court dinking on both sides, the Captain and the Mole won the second game. Score-wise it was close, 12-10. The close score didn't represent the game, though. Fish thought they had been generally outplayed, just a tiny bit, in many points. He thought they could have lost more like 11-7 except for a few good breaks. Plus, near the end, the score 11-10 in favor of the Captain and the Mole, and trying a little too hard, Jon hit an awful serve, unusual in that it went off to the left and out by several feet. This one shot resulted in a crucial side-out, and Mole hit a rare short-angled ace on his serve for the game point.

"Well, you got what you wanted," Jon said between the second and third games. "I'm definitely feeling it now." The queasy feeling was back. The feeling of disconnectedness from his body was growing, although not yet full-bore. He could feel his breathing changing, becoming shallower, up in his chest instead of down in his diaphragm.

"I guess I did at that," agreed Aardvark. "So let's go with it."

*What does that mean, 'go with it'?* Jon wondered. He walked over to the fence. During time-outs either called by a team or between games players can talk to spectators or coaches, so he beckoned Gabby over. She carefully made her way down out of the bleachers, her long legs catching more attention than her outfit, meticulously brushed-out red hair almost mid-back length. Just the sight of her was almost enough. Almost.

"Did you see anything weird about my last serve?" he asked.

"Looked like you turned your whole wrist out. Didn't look like your normal serve at all," she said.

"Any suggestions?"

"Well, maybe one." She reached up and held his shoulders. "Do you remember what I told you at the beginning of the game?"

"I think so. 'Play with today's game'?" Fish said.

"Uh-huh. Maybe you're making more of this than you need to. Maybe, if you're going to move past this now, you could just let your 'anxiety serve' be your serve. After all, you can't really do anything different, can you?"

There was something about the words that made a whole lot of sense. Way more than other sayings. The thing that came closest was 'Dance with the one who brought you,' but he wasn't sure that really was an improvement.

The time-out was over and he walked back onto the court. Gin, the referee, tucked her brown hair back up under a baseball hat and called for the serve. Third game, all the marbles. Of course, if Jon and Aardvark lost they would still have a chance in the loser's bracket, but that would indeed feel like a loss. Jon felt himself growing angry again about Aardvark's having first taken away his backup serve and then taking him out of the zone. Didn't the guy ever want to win a match without doing something weird with it?

Somehow, Jon got the game's first serve in. It was short and ugly, but in. And they lost that point on the Mole's killer get in the back court but could have won it, so that was a plus. That was the last plus Jon saw for a while.

The afternoon was blazing hot. That's the thing about outside courts, Jon thought, no air-conditioning. The afternoon winds hadn't shown up to cool anything down. Jon's sunscreen began melting above his eyebrows and the stuff got in his eyes, causing his bad eye, especially, to lose what vision he had regained. So essentially Jon was playing with one eye, no backhand serve, and a partner who was likely to do anything at any minute. Jon felt it in his gut. They had to lose; they were choosing to set themselves up to lose. He called a time-out, putting the ball under his paddle.

"Man, this is no fun at all," he said. "You got any thoughts?"

"Nope. Just let it play out," said Aardvark.

"Any strategy?"

"Nope." Aardvark wiped his grips down thoroughly with a yellow microfiber cloth. "Did you ever stop to think where we'd be today without microfiber, Velcro, and duct tape?"

Jon smiled. "You gotta add in Sharpies and Post-Its then."

"You wanna try reverse stacking?"

"Sure. Gives 'em something different to look at. Way I feel now, that's better than doing nothing."

For a lefty-righty team, reverse stacking puts backhands in the middle. It's a different look. Initially it didn't help; the white hats dropped another point before getting the serve back. Jon felt all tingly. The reality was he hadn't missed a serve excepting the last one. Which was, really, outstanding for anyone in tournament play. And there was that something Gabby had said, too, that he wanted to think more about. There was too much going on in his mind.

But he needed to get this ball in. He took several calming breaths after the score was called. He tossed the ball. He struck it very cleanly. The ball went straight to about the point of the net, a bit high but serviceable, and then began to veer dramatically to the left. The left line judge watched closely as the ball hit in and within a foot of the back corner. "Nifty," said Aardvark.

"Shithouse luck," Jon said. "Now that I'm this screwed up I have no idea what to do with the next one!" The next serve had the same left veer and went out by the same margin the other had hit in. *Here we go*, Jon thought.

Fortunately, when a player loses his or her serve the rest of their game doesn't suffer too much. Aardvark took the second serve and ran three points, putting them back in the lead.

At this point the stress levels were built to their highest levels for Jon. Aardvark had accomplished what he had tried to do. Now it would take something extraordinary to get Jon's serve back on track. He felt that his head was full of wool. He couldn't think of anything productive. Everything he thought of led to something else. All the workarounds he and Aardvark had worked so hard on were gone, not because they weren't still there, but because he wasn't allowed to use them.

Jon called another time-out. He called Gabby over to the fence.

"Tell me one more time, that last thing you said."

"Play the game you have today," she smiled. "You can do this, but only you."

A light came on. If you have a terrible part of a game and it must be used, figure out how to use it. He looked at the referee. Gin was standing at the back fence watching her stopwatch. In any case Jon had all the time Gin would give him. He went to the service line and closed his eyes. He felt all the cotton in his head. He asked to be shown what lay past the cotton. Images flitted through his mind.

He followed with his breath. Ever so quickly he dropped down and down. He reached a core that spoke to him, that was him. He could see the ball he needed to hit and how. He could see it not with his good eye but with his bad eye. He nodded thankfulness to that entity.

Jon quickly walked over to his bag and grabbed his eye patch. He pushed the patch over so that it covered his good eye, his right eye. His bad eye was still "bad," but he was seeing through it differently than he had before. He nodded thankfulness to the entity that had given him his vision back in this new way.

The other three were in position, looking at him strangely. "Are we gonna play this game or what?" Jon asked, and picked up his paddle.

"Nice look," said the Captain, pointing at his own eye. Jon grinned and snapped the eye patch at his friend.

Fish took the yellow game ball and went to the center of the left serving box. He took two side steps to the left. He turned his body so he was completely outside the court at about the net line. Peripherally he saw people in the stands begin to stand up. Peripherally he saw the cameras begin to roll. Peripherally he saw his opponents, standing with their paddles hanging at their sides, obviously not having the slightest clue what he was doing. And peripherally, but focused in his mind's eye, he saw Gabby, who was standing by little Marie, Gabby's hands crossed over her chest, her watching every move he made.

From the left court Fish had to change his angle so that he was aiming at the outside of the right-hand sideline. He could see clearly with his damaged eye, and he knew what the serve would do. He tossed the ball and hit it with a sharp forehand. It went out of bounds, reversed back and dove down, hitting a little short but deadly.

But let's give credit where credit is due. The Mole got a paddle on it. But still, with that much velocity and sidespin, it flew off his paddle like a fly escaping a fly-swatter. Jon had intentionally hit an ace in a game not known for aces, and all because he simply played with what he had — his own, natural game, as shown to him through a magic eye.

The shot was dramatic. Everybody who saw it was yelling and those that hadn't seen it soon heard enough about it that they came to believe they had seen it, too. With that one shot, Fish added something new to pickleball. But Fish hadn't been trying to invent new shots. He was just getting a serve in. And now he moved to the right court, changed the angle so he was aiming about midway down the court opposite him and hit the same driving and diving serve. The Captain tried to short-hop this one but with the angle, in Fish's mind, that ball could not come back over the net. And in fact, it didn't. He had served two aces in a row with a patch over his good eye.

Aardvark called for their second time-out. "Guess you got the memo, eh?"

Jon grinned. "Guess I did. But you know …"

"Yeah, I know. Let's talk about it later. For right now, let me say that you have arrived. And I don't think you'll fear making any serve anytime soon."

"Hadn't thought about the arriving part. But what do we do now?" Jon was truly puzzled. "I think I could serve out on 'em with that serve, but what would that prove?"

"And that's why we really play this game, isn't it? We want their best game!"

"Why don't we just play the rest of the match straight up? No weird serves but no restrictions either?"

"Done!" said Aardvark. "Maybe you could take off the eyepatch, too!"

With only two players to play against now, instead of

three with him in the way, the game was over in fifteen minutes. Maybe the big news was that Jon had finally met his enemy and found a way through the biggest block in his sports career: himself. It seemed that something in him had shifted and his ever-present anxiety had gone, leaving him focused, alert, and interested in the game. Paradoxically, the last point came on Aardvark's serve. He hit an absolute dishrag of a serve, a nothing-burger, a ball that was in but short, and had no power and no planned intention.

The Mole stepped up and swung very early and whiffed the ball completely, so completely he tried to run behind it to hit it again. With his quickness he got to it, but just too late and couldn't get the ball back in bounds. The Mole was grinning and applauding on the way to the net. As did the crowd of spectators covering every inch of viewing space around the courts.

The meeting at the net was one of old friends, all congratulating each other. And as Aardvark would later say to Jon, this match was what pickleball was about, a way to connect with your friends, your family, a way to have fun and through fun to learn something, sometimes, about yourself.

Gabby was leaning on the fence next to the gate when Fish finally left the court. Ray was with her, sitting, leash trailing, a quiet dog for once. He ruffed Ray's neck and took Gabby into a huge bear hug that lasted a long time.

Aardvark came through. "Get a room," he grinned.

Gabby turned to him and hugged him, in turn. "Thanks for everything, you beautiful man," she said.

"Wow. I bet that's the first time anybody's called you beautiful," Jon said, watching.

"I don't remember many others," admitted the Aardvark. "But I do make it a point to call myself beautiful at least once a day." He kissed the back of his own hairy hand, winked at Jon and Gabby and walked away.

Back in their hug, Jon looked down at Gabby. "When are we going to talk?"

"We're talking right now." She looked up at him. "But as to that thing …"

"Your leaving?" Jon clarified.

"… would you mind if we wait until tonight? I can explain more easily then."

Jon had no desire to wait at all. If there was something amiss, or, worse, something afoot, he wanted to know. And then … *all about control*, he thought. *I don't need that now*. The cloud lifted again and he nodded.

# Chapter Thirty-Four

THERE IS A FAIR AMOUNT of waiting time between the finish of this last match in the winner's bracket, which of course was Jon and Aardvark, and the winner of the Bronze match in the consolation bracket.

With Pit Bull now somewhat healthy, he and Three-Dog were heavily favored to win that match in spite of their earlier loss to the same team, the Captain and the Mole. But it needed to be played out. The Captain and the Mole were obviously a top team today; nobody would — or at least should — take them lightly. Still, the Bronze-match game went predictably. With PB able to move and able to hit the ball through concrete, the Captain and the Mole had no choice, they had to stay away from him.

But Three-Dog hadn't gotten there on his dapper good looks alone; his game revolved around misdirection, especially hitting through the middle with the most unlikely looking backhands. And once an opponent caught on to that, he'd begin to fake right and go left from anywhere on the court, it didn't matter. The opponents would still be chasing the balls to the sidelines, putting the balls back up if they could get to them at all, and PB would slide over and just rocket the put-aways.

Watching from the fence, Jon knew these guys were the other top two in the bracket, along with the Aard and him. Overall, he and Aard had more variety in their game, but he respected PB and Three-Dog. He thought they were a little too predictable, running that one set play over and over again if they could. But they were the team he wanted to play. If he was gonna win this tournament, he would go through the best teams and not limp in. Not really to prove anything, just because that was the most fun.

The first game finished up 11-7 for PB and Three-Dog. Jon turned and noticed Aardvark, only half-watching the match from the aluminum bleachers. Mostly he was staring into the sky.

Jon came up the steps and sat with him. "What?" he said, nodding up.

"Rain," Aardvark said, still looking at the cloudless sky.

"Always a possibility in Bend," Jon said cheerfully. "Doesn't look much like it now."

Bend is high desert, and thunderstorms are often in the forecast. They come and go quickly, never amounting to more than a momentary drenching during the summer, just enough to cool things off "... or get the courts totally wet," Fish realized.

"There's something else," the A said, nodding toward the new game. "Look at PB."

Jon turned to look at his other friend. While PB and Three-Dog had early points and were clearly under control, PB was definitely not moving well. One of his characteristics, beyond his exceptional power, was his side-to-side reaction time, which was way above average. Except right now. Compared to his norm, he was rapidly becoming fixed in place like a signpost in a drying bucket of concrete.

"It's that hip again, isn't it?" Fish asked. "Can you fix it again?"

"Probably, but not for good," said the Aardvark. "If it's

come out again so quickly there's nothing holding it in place. Bone on bone."

"The powers only go so far, huh?"

"Yep," the muscular Aard said succinctly. "Can't create something from nothing."

"We could hope for a rain delay," said Jon. "This late in the day a delay would take us into tomorrow. You could try to patch him again. And maybe the rest would do him good."

"Well, looks like we'll find out."

Anne, the tournament director, had come up into the stands and sat down between Aardvark and Jon. "It's gonna rain pretty soon," she said definitively, looking up at the still-clear sky. The winds had continued to pick up and Jon thought it did smell a bit rain-like.

"What are you gonna do?" he asked her.

Anne was tall, a, long-legged, good-looking blonde not showing her sixty years. When she turned to him he noticed she was wearing a small bronze earring that had the same symbol embossed on it as his earring ... a circle with what looked like a small snake wrapped around it. He reached over and flicked it gently with a fingernail. "Nice," he said, looking across her at Aardvark.

"Well, I did tell you I knew her." Aard put a meaty arm around the woman and gave her a friendly squeeze.

She smiled at Aard and turned back to Jon. "It'll now rain in ... 29 minutes," she said. "We'll never get the courts dry after, not this late in the afternoon. It'll be dark before they're dry."

She looked out at the match in front. "Lucky for 'ol PB and Three-Dog," she added. "PB is hurtin' for certain." Their opponents had picked up on PB's increasing slowness and were now playing him to the sides, making him move. Smart play but PB and Three-Dog were playing it smart as well. They were forcing the ball to whichever side PB was on, making their opponents always come direct across the net, instead of being able to work the more difficult-to-handle angles. PB, in turn, was resorting to less wide cross-court dinking, instead, often dropping the ball softly over the net in the middle or going directly opposite him to his opponent in order to cut down their opportunities and to give Three-Dog a chance to get in the act.

Both teams kept shifting their efforts, looking for advantage. But overall, the score in the game was going similarly to the first, with each point for PB and Three-Dog almost a visible relief. There were lots more low-fives and lots more chatter between them, Three-Dog keeping the mercurial PB calm and under control.

"Fifteen minutes," Anne said, looking up. "They'll finish on time, I think."

Jon looked up. The sky was, in fact, darkening where only fifteen minutes before it had been virtually clear. "How do you do that?" he asked her. She smiled and touched her earring. "Oh," he said. "That's useful!"

As Anne had forecasted the game ended in just under fifteen minutes. The score was the same as in the second game, 11-7, but it had been a much harder-fought battle. This game had been a grind; it was still hot and the players were showing it. The Captain grabbed his water bottle and dunked it over his head. The Mole picked up his stuff, hugged his friends quickly, and headed for cover. The Aard went to the fence and collected Pit Bull, bringing him to a nearby flat patch of grass under a tree and making him comfortable on a blanket Jon had snagged from the medical team.

Jon watched interestedly as Aardvark worked PB up into a side-laying position, put a thick hand on his hip, balanced himself and gradually leveraged his weight up so that most of his considerable weight was on the hip-joint in a one-handed pushup position. The move itself was stellar, something only a very experienced yoga practitioner would try to do. He simply held that position for quite a while, perhaps a full minute, after which everyone gathered could hear the audible 'click' of PB's hip popping itself back into place. PB had put his hand over his mouth, knowing what was coming, but even still his grunt was discernable from yards around.

Aardvark pulled PB up onto his feet as if he were a feather and gave him a hug. "That'll make you feel quite a bit better," he said, looking into PB's eyes. "I'll assume it'll get you through our match. Which, with the rain, will be tomorrow."

"I would have played now if my leg was falling off," said PB, who didn't like needing help. "We'll kick your butt tomorrow."

Three-Dog smiled at Aardvark. "Thanks," he said.

The Aard simply bowed. "My pleasure," he said. "Remember to have your partner ice that hip."

The skies opened up and further conversation, by mutual agreement, was postponed.

The evening was relatively uneventful, spent as per their norm over at the pond until too late to see, then into their coaches. Ray had decided that riding in the golf cart was even better than hunting frogs and with Eddie as his chauffer was gone for hours, but was back in Fish's coach before he was, having mastered the trick of opening the screen door.

Gabby and Fish had not talked out her absence that day or the meaning of it. By some mutual agreement, it appeared to be less important to both of them. At one point, Gabby did mention at that it was still an open issue.

"I know you don't like loose ends," she said. "I want you to know we can talk through that anytime. We can talk through anything, anytime."

"We'll get to it," Fish said, unrolling her sleeping bag onto the couch loveseat.

Gabby watched him for a minute. "Know what?" she asked. "I think I'd rather sleep on the big-boy bed tonight."

"The couch is a little small for me," Fish said.

"I know." The edges of Gabby's mouth turned up and her eyes shined. "And we wouldn't want that ..."

"True," was all Fish could think of to say. But he did think to hold her hand the three steps toward the bedroom.

Bend has many gorgeous days every year, days when the world is in balance, when anything is possible. The next morning was one of those days, with a blue-bird sky and windless. Fish was outside doing sun salutations, Ray pretending to sleep up on the picnic table. Gabby came out and watched her lover for a moment. "You're pretty graceful for a tall guy," she said.

Fish looked at her, still wearing a nightshirt, hair disheveled, more beautiful than any woman ever has been. He grinned evilly. "You aren't so bad yourself," he said.

"You just love me for my body," Gabby answered, running her fingers through her tousled hair like a comb.

"It doesn't hurt," he smiled. "That's only one of the things I love about you."

A few hours later they were at Pine Nursery and Fish was ready to do battle. An hour or more out from being called, he was already getting pumped. Anyone who plays tournament pickleball loves those times when the gods grant them the chance to play in a gold medal match. The rarity of playing a gold medal match as the first match of the day, with everyone rested and wounds mostly bandaged if not healed, is a special treat. Folks were milling about waiting.

Anne came over. "Good crowd," she said to the three.

Aardvark looked around at a throng of people. "You know, I never notice the crowd," he said. "Sometimes individuals, but not the crowd."

There are many factors that make a good match great. Even pairings, of course. That's usually a function of good seeding within the bracket and the average amount of luck going around. You don't always have even pairings in the final round, but it happened more often than not in Jon's admittedly limited experience. Ability to win is another factor. Some teams find a way through, no matter what. Both teams, Jon thought, were pretty darn good at that. Court conditions can always be a factor, although in this case, being the day after a rain and thanks to the amazing court crew who had used the rain, the courts looked pretty darn sparkly as well.

Another factor is familiarity. When Jon played the same team over and over again, he could more easily see the weaknesses and exploit them more regularly with less thought or effort. That was true here. PB played more often with Camino against Aard and Jon, and less often with Three-Dog, but previous commitments had caused the change in line-up. What did Jon know about Three-Dog? Quite a bit, but not at the same level he 'got' Camino, one of the smoothest players around, but to some extent one of the more predictable as well. Three-Dog was later in his career, one of the few players still competitive over age seventy who had three great shots Jon noted were working yesterday. One was a backhand punch through the middle. Somehow Three-Dog could hit that thing from just about any body position. The second was his deceptive sideline shot, drilling the ball opposite of where he was looking. That was always a problem for Fish.

The third shot Jon worried a bit about was his lob. While he hadn't used it much yesterday, beating Captain and Mole more with the sideline and center shots, his lob was amazing, and he could hit it from deep as well as from the line. Jon and Aard were not the easiest players to lob against but they couldn't discount a strength. The open question was if Three-Dog could execute the shot against a team that had height and reach (Jon) as well as quickness and commanding power (Aard). Jon thought they'd be okay defending against Three-Dog's lob. Three-Dog would have to get it over Fish to begin with; Fish had a great overhead brought forward from his tennis days, and the Aard could always run it down if it got by Fish.

Jon went over to Aard, who was massaging his calf muscle. "You okay?" asked Jon.

"Perfect," said Aard. "I'm just messin' with PB a little bit!" He nodded slightly toward their opponents who were watching Aard work on his calf. "Don't know if they'll believe my act or not."

"No, they won't," said Fish. "Not after you got PB put back together. I think they think you can fix anything."

"Physician, heal thyself?" asked the Aardvark. "Not always possible."

"Yeah, but they probably think you can." Jon began his pre-match stretches. He felt remarkably limber today, even after a medium run with Ray much earlier. His body felt light. Very little was weighing him down. He still wondered about that lob, though, so he mentioned it to Aardvark.

"Thing about that lob," said the Aard, "is that for it to be effective over you it's got to be both sky-high and deep. And if he does that, it'll take more time than his normal lob and I can get back and cover it."

Jon thought about that. His friend was right. In all probability, Three-Dog had more to worry about to make the lob work than he did to cover it. In any event, they would soon see. Their gold medal match was being played on Court Fifteen, which had a great setup for cameras as well as tons of aluminum bleacher seating. The bleachers were already filling up, the air temperature was nice at about 60 degrees, and it looked like 'go' time.

The announcer had a true radio voice, deep and almost romantic. Strange term to use for a court announcement. "We have our first gold medal match of the day! On Court Fifteen, in the Men's 4.0, we have the Aardvark and Fish playing against Pit Bull and Three-Dog. We will need ... (this slurred) ... the Back-Liner line judge team. Please report to Court Fifteen."

With the court called for the match, it was cleared for the teams to begin warm-ups. Jon went over to the fence and looked for Gabby. He spotted her right away, top row and hard to miss, especially with back-lit hair on fire, looking like a commercial — and flash — there Jon was, running across some random field somewhere, and she was running to him. She threw herself to him in the scene and he turned her round and round, her white dress flowing with her ... *YOW!* Jon thought to himself. *Head in game!*

Aardvark walked over. "What say you? Shall we hit a few?"

Jon grinned. "Guess so. It's why we're here."

The natural beauty of Pine Nursery Park and the pristine setting of the pickleball courts seemed spectacular to Fish on this glorious day. Everything seemed bright and glowing.

271

The outfits pickleball players wear are often an additional point of interest. Today Fish and Aardvark were each wearing their traditional go-to playing garb. The Aard wore his personal game shirt, the brown shirt with another vague Aardvark inside of it and so on, each one smaller than the one before, reaching to an infinity of aardvarks. He also wore his Walmart orange shorts, shiny-clean black and white high-top shoes, dark ribbed dress socks, the whole megillah, just like he had worn in Palm Creek the first time Jon had seen him. His robe completed his outfit and, ready to warm up, he threw it over the fence to Anne who in turn tossed it up in the stands to Gabby. Jon wore his taupe Zen design shirt and blue cotton gym shorts but with his killer metallic shoes, shoes no one else out there except Fish would wear.

Then came Pit Bull and Three-Dog. Seeing them, Fish almost laughed out loud. He thought there should have been a clarion call or something to announce them; Three-Dog and Pit Bull were in matching outfits, in the reddest outfits Fish had ever seen. Everything about them was red. Unfortunately, red wasn't either of their color. Three-Dog's face looked washed out. It was worse with Pit Bull, because of his size. He was wide, not quite as thick as Aardvark but somewhere in there, and the contrast between all that red-ness; his red hat, his red shoes, his red laces, and his paddle with a red edge guard, and the earth tones of the court was striking, to say the least. Jon, still trying his best not to laugh, continued to stare at him. Pit Bull stared back at him malevolently. "What are you looking at?" he asked.

"I'm not sure," said Fish. "I'd like to come up with a good one-liner here and I'm sure I'll think of something later, but right now all I can think of is a crab. A huge, red crab."

Pit Bull glared. "Happy wife, happy life," he said. "His," he pointed to Three-Dog. He snapped his claw-hands at

Fish. "Gonna make crab salad out of you two," he said.

"Oh, gotcha," said Fish, still grinning. Three-Dog's wife had a thing about outfits and had tried to get him into stuff like this before, although Fish couldn't remember her successes being this dramatic. Three-Dog was known to be red-green color blind anyway and undoubtedly could care less. But it certainly was an attraction. No, Fish rethought. A DIS-traction. He glanced over at Aardvark who was also staring at the pair. "We could have done that," said Fish.

"No, I don't think we could have," said Aardvark. "Or at least we never will."

Warmups were finished and the match referee, a very seasoned certified referee named Ivy, gave instructions and set them in their places. Jon and Aardvark had won the coin flip and chose to serve.

"Any last-minute thoughts?" asked Jon as they walked to their places.

"Nope," said Aard. "We're ready for this."

Jon thought about that. He agreed, yeah, they probably were. And they might have an advantage. Coming up from the consolation bracket as they were, Pit Bull and Three-Dog would need to beat Jon and Aard twice to win gold. They'd first have to win two of the first three 11-point games, and then would need to win a tie-breaker to 15 points and by a two-point margin. That favored the white-hats, Fish thought.

He wasn't gonna take that to the bank, though, that overconfidence wasn't his way. It's not uncommon to have the consolation bracket winners come out with gold. Yes, it's less likely, one theory being that by the time the consolation bracket winners play the winners' bracket winners, they have often played many more games and the losers' bracket folks might have an endurance issue.

273

But if that's an advantage at all it certainly didn't apply here as everyone had a good night's sleep … well, as good a night's sleep as you can have when it's all on the line the next morning. In fact, Pit Bull looked remarkably spry, and was making a point of doing stretching exercises his hip wouldn't have allowed him to think about making yesterday afternoon.

They were in position now. Aardvark looked over. "You've come a long way, grasshoppah," he said.

Fish grinned. He was feeling it now, and his first serve went dead center of the correct court and within a foot of the baseline. Cool, he thought. Let's roll.

If there was ever a Hall of Fame for 4.0 players and a match that qualified them, every spectator would remember this match and write it in for consideration. There were two- and even three-minute segments given over to the match that night on local television. What made it so memorable? More than anything else it was the same things done well over and over again. Within seconds of the first ball being in play, Aardvark put the ball up a bit and the red Pit Bull slid over to hammer it at Fish's chest. Fish was ready and remarkably, the ball, seen through the prism of his two eyes, was, in fact, simply slower than it had been the day before. He just put his paddle up, received the body slam with the paddle coming back a fraction toward him, and dinked it back to the surprised Pit Bull. This in turn caused the Bull to dink a bit too high to Aard who returned it hard at the feet of Three-Dog, who dug it up on a short hop and hit the first lob of the day, a short looper designed to get over Fish.

The ball was a bit short, however, and Fish caught up with it well before the baseline, ran around the shot and dropped it to the waiting Pit Bull's backhand. The Pit allowed the ball to come up and hit a great dink into the 'safe' horseshoe-shaped area that extends out from the middle of the net about two feet. 'Safe' because the shot will cause most teams to trip over themselves deciding on who is supposed to go in and get it, and further because there's not much one can do with it. Unless you are Fish, today, who came in and did an ultra-soft dink back again, a shot designed to go nowhere at all and to bounce only the minimum that physics will tell you a plastic whiffle-type-ball has to bounce. Both Pit and Three-Dog went after that one, clacked paddles, and the first point went to the white-hats.

To describe every point in this game would require listing every shot ever hit in pickleball. Of the four players, Fish was undoubtedly the most theatrical, however, and as Gabby told him later, he hit shots that day that she had never seen him hit. The four around the post put-aways, the outside the post back corner shots, the crossing lobs; he had the whole game. Interestingly, Aardvark called Jon in on far more shots than he normally did, and each time he did, irrespective of result, he would tap his paddle appreciatively as Jon took each cue and dispensed with it.

As good a pair of players as they were, making heroic digs and pounding the put-aways and doing all the things making up the list of excellent efforts, nothing worked for Pit Bull and Three-Dog. They had nothing they could mount against the relentless attack that the Aard and Jon had. Not to say they didn't have their moments; they did. But the first game was all white-hat, 11-6, a rout among close pairings like these.

The second game started out much more in the Pit Bull-Three-Dog corner, but Jon and Aard quickly erased Pit's three-point first serve run on the side out and never really looked back. The second game was a long one, time wise, each player fighting for everything he could contribute. Aardvark alone took something of a back seat, deferring to his student whenever he could. The deference added to their partnering and what they had was more than enough. One reason that the people in the winners' bracket often win gold is because they are the best team. Everybody on the court and off knew that that was Fish and Aardvark. Fish was the near-perfect player, and the Aard was the nearly perfect partner.

But right then, the play was the thing and they simply needed to finish the match. On what possibly would be the very last point of the game with Fish serving, he looked over to Aardvark and winked. He received back a one thousand-watt grin showing every one of those alligator teeth. Fish took the ball, tossed it, and simply put it in play to within two feet from the back line, as if he had been doing it all his life, as if there was nothing to it at all. And three shots later, when Pit Bull was about to drop the ball into the kitchen, Fish glanced at his feet, reached in, took it out of the air, flipped it over the head of Three-Dog in the most perfect Enrique lob ever, and the game was over.

There were back-breaking hugs and some high fives at the net. Pit Bull looked at Fish, no expression at all. "We couldn't have beaten you today," he said. Three-Dog nodded. "Especially with you backing the guy up," he said to Aardvark, white teeth and hair flashing against the crab-red outfit. "You owned us."

Aardvark bowed slightly. "Nice of you to say, but there are still many areas where we could improve."

Pit looked over. "Not in this bracket there isn't," he said.

Fish smiled to himself as that sunk in. He had killed a major demon today and might soon have a chance to put that to the test in a different bracket; who knows? From Pit Bull's lips to God's ear! He had done his part at least. And the gods could do theirs, when they were ready. All pretty much part of His plan, after all.

As he put his gear together to leave the court, Fish thought more about what Three-Dog had said, about the role Aardvark had played and realized that what Three-

Dog said was truth. He had had the gift of a perfect partner. If there was ever a textbook partner for someone who was on fire like Fish, it was Aardvark. Further, he did it with such delight. Fish instantly remembered how pleased Aardvark had been with the fellow who had given him a good skunking in singles in Palm Creek a thousand years ago. He had been just that delighted then, and in his own mind Fish knew that Aardvark had done, in this match, what he intended, and had given Fish a gift he could take with him forever.

Outside the gate, Fish was besieged by well-wishers and fellow players, but took a moment to go over to Aardvark. "I saw you today," Fish said. "Who you were out there. Thanks."

Aardvark adjusted his robe. "You are more than welcome, friend Fish. Early on said we could walk some of the Middle Path together, if you remember. Today was another step, I think."

Fish was surprised to see Sam approach them. "Well, you picked a better match to watch," he said.

Sam put his arm around his friend. "You know, you are definitely the son I never wanted to have," he said, grinning. "But you sure can play pickleball when your head isn't in your ass!"

Aardvark grinned. "On those rare occasions," he said.

Raphael came up as well. "Okay, so now I get it, pickleball," he said. "I loved that. But I'm gonna beat you like a rented mule by next year!"

"Wow," Fish said. "And you've already got the trash-talk working!"

While they were chatting, Anne came up to Fish and Aardvark, holding the elbow of a trim grey-haired man with coke-bottle glasses. "This is Tom Christos," she said, pushing him forward. "He wanted to talk with you guys."

"You would be that Tom Christos?" Fish said.

Tom smiled. "If you mean am I the ratings chair, then, yes, I am," he said. "And I've agreed with Anne, you two need to go up. We're putting you both at 4.5 in the next ratings round in a couple of months."

Jon was surprised. Aardvark didn't look surprised, but with him, thought Jon, who knows? In any case, a lot of hard work had gone into this, and although it happened pretty quickly, Jon was comfortable with it. Strangely, moving to a higher bracket didn't seem to mean as much to him as he had thought it would. That was just another goal, another mark on the board. To him now, the play was the thing. Well, the play and the family; his own family perhaps and the pickleball family, too, a very real thing.

Anne and Tom walked off and Gabby was there, another quick splash of sunshine. "Congrats, big guy," she said to Fish. She punched the Aard on the shoulder, and not too lightly, either.

"Ow! Did you ever tell Jon why you had to leave?" the Aardvark asked, rubbing his shoulder bone where she had hit him.

"Not yet. We were going to talk and didn't. But why don't you tell him? It was your idea."

Fish looked at the two of them. "Yeah, you said it was. What's up with that?"

Aardvark looked around. For the moment, they were alone. "Here it is," he said, taking a small box out of his pocket. He handed it to Fish. "To be honest, I wanted you to be under a little extra pressure for the tournament, so that was part of it, Gabby helping with that. But here's the other part."

Fish turned it over. It looked like a small jewelry box, but it was wood and carved, stained red and unwrapped.

"I wouldn't have agreed if it was just the pressure part," said Gabby. "A bit too manipulative for this girl, especially because it was you. And Fish ..." she came up to him and put her arms around his neck, "... I'm really, really sorry it caused you some pain. I hope you can forgive me for that. But I did think this was pretty cool."

Fish kissed her lightly. "I forgave you the minute I saw you again," he said. "I don't know why, but I did. I usually hold a grudge. Maybe you're special or something."

He opened the little box. Inside was a bronze ring. It had a design on the polished surface unlike anything he had seen. It was reminiscent of what Fish had come to think of as the snake in the earring but not quite. It was more intricate, elaborate and at the same time, unfinished, the design open on one edge like an opening into a maze. There was a tiny irregular black stone at one edge of the oval surface. It was both fluid and airy in its design, altogether the most attractive ring Fish had seen.

"This is awesome!" he said to Gabby, turning it over and over in his palm. He loved the weight of it. "But why do I get it?"

"I don't know," she said, "but I have one, too!" She held up her right hand. Her ring was virtually identical, except, fittingly, more delicate overall. The stone in the surface of her ring was a very deep red. They put the two rings next to each other. The unfinished edges of each matched into and completed the design.

Fish put his on and held it up. Even though it was bright out in the mid-morning sun, the whole of the ring held light and color and the stone, dark as it was, had flashes inside it. Too cool for school!

"I made those for you two quite a while ago," interjected Aardvark. "I had left them over in Albany to have one of our gang work and set the stones."

"There wasn't even any 'two of us' until recently," Jon said. "How did you know?"

"Raphael told me," he said, "although it was clear as day even before that, that something was headed your way. Or that you were headed for something. It had an aura like a tsunami."

"Thanks so much," Jon said. "Really, it's too much."

"No. It's more something the two of you might need," Aardvark said.

Jon and Gabby looked at each other, then at the very self-satisfied Aard. "Think you might want to share a little more?"

"Oh, sure," said the Aardvark. "Tonight?"

## Chapter Thirty-Five

IT WAS THEIR LAST EVENING at the Bend-Sisters RV Park. Fish and Aard were once again out at the pond under the stars, and Gabby was strolling around the pond's backside with Ray, letting the young boxer get one last shot at a frog, her dog, Jersey, trying to help, slipping in and out of the water.

"Great tournament," said Aardvark, lighting a joint.

"Great tournament," Fish agreed, taking the blunt. "Couldn't even imagine one being more fun. Especially going through Pit and Three-Dog in the last match. Super sweet."

Aard took the joint back. "Pretty sure his hip is history," he reflected. "But he's a tough cookie. He'll be back soon." He glanced sideways at Jon. "On another matter, though, I'm heading down the road tomorrow. But I'm feeling a little lonely already. You grow on a person, as strange as you are."

"Look who's talking," Jon said. "I think your picture is in the dictionary under 'weird.'"

"I wanted to talk a little about that," Aardvark said, ignoring the last. "Share some stuff."

Gabby was back and pulled up a chair. Fish scratched Ray's ruff and turned to her. Aardvark offered the joint to her. She declined and he flicked the roach out into the lake. "So there's stuff I need to share," he said. "I mean, so you don't label me cryptic and all."

He adjusted the worn camp chair so he faced the two of them. They had set a small fire and the shadows danced on his rugged face as he talked.

"First, about the powers and all. I've told you, Fish, and maybe you both, that I view the powers as a natural extension of the work we do to find ourselves. Usually there's something you're trying to overcome and the effort brings you outside yourself somehow. The struggle redefines your nature, in a way.

"There's a lot more to it than that. Right Intention, Right Action are somehow involved, too. But not in the defined Buddhist way, of course. Here, if one perseveres they generally 'Arrive,' as we call it. It's probably less of a transformative awakening than a sudden sure knowledge that there is more to us as individuals than meets the eye. And the more we continue to work at it, the more receptive we are to these changes. We drop our resistance to change. We even allow challenges to our core beliefs, which is a very heavy lift."

Fish felt like he should raise his hand like in a classroom but thought the better of it. "So we don't know, really, how to get to this 'Arrival' except to keep working at it. Nor do we know exactly what will occur."

Behind them, they saw the pull of headlights entering the campground, coming toward them. They watched casually as the car carefully picked its way down the row. A man stepped out. In the feeble light, Aardvark recognized him. "Sam," he said. "I was hoping he'd come by."

Sam came up, still walking a bit gingerly and carrying a camp chair. He pulled up into the group.

"What did I miss?" he asked Aardvark.

"Talking about powers, is all," answered the Aard. "I was about to say that it's pretty much guaranteed, that as long as you do the work, you'll arrive somewhere and a power you didn't know you had will be yours for the using. Could be anything, though, and usually they show up with limitations."

"Limitations." Gabby said definitively. "What limitations?"

"Well, like yesterday. I couldn't really fix PB's hip so it would stay past our match, even though healing is one of my things."

"Or like my sight!" Fish realized. "The main thing I do with it right now is slow the ball down. That gives me a kind of on demand in the zone-ness. But it only goes so far."

"Right, exactly. Each of the attributes comes with some limitations. But not to worry, the power grows over time. That's the other thing." Aardvark scraped a couple of stones over to him with his bare foot and began plunking them at a small log floating in the pond, barely visible in the gloaming.

"Whattaya think will happen with my eyesight?" Jon said. "It's still not real useful in that eye except for that slowing-the-ball-down trick."

"It's not a trick," Aardvark said calmly, "but there's no knowing. I suspect with you, it's so early, it'll get stronger somehow. But what that means, we can't tell yet."

Gabby had obviously been thinking about something. "What does this have to do with our new rings?" she asked.

"You're getting me off track, but the rings are an experiment. I'm thinking maybe they'll be an amplifier. If they work the way I hope they will, they'll enhance each of your powers sooner. Take both of you past your 10 per cent limit, maybe."

"I suppose we'd have to be, like, touching?" Fish held Gabby's hand so her ring was next to his. "They seem to fit together, sort of."

"Is that a problem, darling?" Gabby asked in a saccharine voice, taking her hand away. "Touching?"

Fish looked at her and smiled. He even loved her edges.

Aardvark smiled benevolently. "They are designed to complete each other. Maybe nearness would be enough, but I think touching would be better."

Sam looked over. "Hey, Fish. Did you ever figure out what I can do?"

"No clue," he said. "Other than not be a very good psychiatrist?"

"I'm hurt," said Sam. "But you should have figured it out. Those drawings I made for you?"

"You're a crappy artist ... that's a power?"

"I choose to ignore that comment, too. The cards are like mental Post-Its, but a step above. They connect the person who gets the picture — you in this case — to a future action or person. It's cool when it works."

For Jon a light finally turned on with a huge mental flash. "O-o-o-K!" Fish said. "You draw those pictures on those cards ..."

"... like the first card, I was actually looking at a photograph of Aardvark and my son ... it works better that way ..." added Sam.

"... and it brought Aardvark and me together, huh?"

Sam smiled. "Yeah, I don't know one word for what it is. A portal? Maybe a door? A magnet? Doesn't always work, though. But sometimes the cards work like a charm, so to speak."

Fish looked at him. "That card with the tree. What's that

one about?"

Sam looked back at him. "Don't know yet. Let's wait and see."

"If that's enough to start with, would y' all want to go back to my motor home?" asked the A. "It'd be warmer sitting inside."

They packed up their chairs, turned on flashlights, and wandered the dirt path back to the A's pristine motor home, gleaming now even in the near-complete dark.

Looking at the RV's glow, Jon wondered out loud. "How do you make that thing shine in the dark? Powers?"

"Walbernese RV Super Wax," Aardvark answered. "Might even make you look good."

Sam grinned. "There isn't that much wax in the world." Jon gave him the look. "Hey, I'm just sayin'," the psychiatrist said, very pleased with himself.

On the subject of truly cool RVs, Jon reflected, Airstreams are amazing. Far more can fit in them than anyone should expect, including, in this case, several people and two dogs. Ray curled up on the small rug near the door and Jersey curled up next to Ray. Airstreams are also remarkably safe-feeling, like being in a beautiful airplane and floating on air. Jon immediately felt even more secure, if that was possible.

Aardvark bustled around and soon had tea in front of each of them. He turned the accent lights on around the interior of the small home and lit two candles.

"I'm interested in what you think about your own plan now," said Sam.

Fish had been thinking about that himself, off and on. "I don't know. I think these months have been amazing. But I'm not sure how they track with the plan, if at all."

Sam leaned in. "Can you think of it in terms of goals met or unmet?"

Fish looked at his shrink and friend. "I had several things going on when I put that plan together, right? Hated my job, hated my family, hated my lack of family, didn't want to be in Bend any more, wanted to become something I wasn't ... like a professional pickleball player ... lots of stuff."

"Yes, you did," Sam agreed, wafting some of the candle smoke toward himself and sniffing it. "Nice smell," he observed to Aardvark, who nodded.

"So if I turned my discontent into goals, this has been a screaming success." Fish looked at each of them in turn. "I found a friend. Well, friends. I found a woman who I bet is gonna be in this thing with me for a good long while" ('A life sentence,' Gabby whispered to herself, flushing) "and I met most of my objectives for making this a better world for myself. Not to mention inheriting a whole family ... the pickleball family, I mean. That's pretty cool, isn't it?"

"Never met a pickleball player I didn't like," agreed Aardvark, listening intently. "But you hit on a key point when you talked about making it a better world."

"What do you mean?" asked Gabby, leaning against Fish's shoulder and looking intently at Aardvark.

"Think about it. If Arriving comes with an increase in our capabilities and if that can be seen as a gift, what's the purpose of the gift? How should we use it?"

Fish thought about it. "You mean there's a price to be paid? You told me I shouldn't help unless people ask for it."

"Right," said Aardvark. "And I mean this in the nicest possible way, but this is truly a difficult time in our world. There is so much polarization, so many sides to every issue, so little working together on anything. If we as a race are meant to survive, there has to be a way to break through those barriers, to break them down. The powers show up when we do the work, and we get past that 10 percent barrier Sam always talks about. Sometimes I think the powers are given to us so that we can do more, assuming people want that."

Fish looked at him. "What you are talking about is finding people we can help by working with them? One at a time?"

"Sort of," said Aardvark.

"Do you see that as what we do?" asked Sam.

"Well, not exactly," Aard said, adjusting his robe. "I think the object is for each of us to get past that ten percent barrier if there is one. To get there, I think we each have a path to follow. In some cases we can follow on a path with one of our fellow suffering humans. And maybe that will be enough to set that one person on a better path." He pointed at Fish. "You said it worked with you," he said. "Maybe now you just find one other person and share with him or her, the way I shared with you."

*Share!* Fish remembered the meditation session. It'd been weeks since he'd thought of that word. But he had an issue. "I don't have your skills," he said simply.

"Don't need them. What you have now is a great foundation. You're getting to be an expert on Fish. Maybe you can use that foundation to help someone else pour theirs. When the time is right to share what you have."

Gabby turned to look at Fish. "I think he's saying that this person will appear for you. And in the meantime, we should live our lives."

"As well as you can," Aardvark agreed. "The universe gave you to me," he added. "There's every reason to suspect the universe will give someone else to you."

Gabby looked at Fish. "If you don't want to wait for the universe to reveal someone, you could start sharing with me now, you know."

Fish smiled at her and started to get up. "I don't think so," he said. "I have more immediate plans for you."

"Oh, please, get a room," said the Aardvark. "And anyway, Gabby is next on my list. Find your own person."

## About the Author

A.J. HAS PUBLISHED numerous short stories, including many articles on pickleball for Pickleball.Biz, and Pickleball Magazine. He holds a masters degree in Creative Writing from Antioch University.

A.J. was president of the Palm Creek Pickleball Club and one of the founders and president of the Bend Pickleball Club. He has been a District USAPA Ambassador, was Director of Training at Palm Creek Pickleball Club, Ratings Chair at Palm Creek, and more.

He and his wife, Irene, and their dogs, Desi and Buster, live equally in Casa Grande, Arizona and Bend, Oregon and in a 36-foot Winnebago Journey, enjoying their passions for pickleball and fly-fishing. They have two sons, one daughter, and four grandchildren.

The family is currently moving to St. George, Utah, which will be part of the setting for the next volume in *The Fish Finder Chronicles*. This is his second novel.

Should you wish to share your thoughts regarding anything gleaned from this book, please drop a line to: pickleballbiz@gmail.com.

www.ingramcontent.com/pod-product-compliance
Lightning Source LLC
Chambersburg PA
CBHW060008050426
42448CB00012B/2669